GAME BIRD HUNTING.

F. Philip Rice
and
John I. Dahl

OUTDOOR LIFE • FUNK & WAGNALLS
New York

Contents

1

Ducks

Of all the birds we hunt on the North American continent, ducks probably provide the most sport for the most hunters. The sport of duck hunting is also the most diverse, and can be the most complicated of all our shotgunning sports. This, of course, is not true in all areas of the country. In the sparsely populated areas where ducks congregate in huge numbers during the fall, scarcely more than a shotgun and a pair of hip boots are needed to take a limit of ducks. In most parts of the country, however, successful duck hunting involves some complicated gunning rigs and equipment. For this reason, duck hunters are usually either "dyed-in-the-wool" types who go about their sport seriously and scientifically, or those who take a shot at a duck on opening day, and thereafter only when the chance presents itself while hunting other game.

It could be said that duck hunting is the traditional shotgunning sport of the United States. Many of the pioneers and early homesteaders lived mainly on duck flesh during the times of the year when the birds were plentiful, and during the nineteenth century, many professional hunters made their livings shooting waterfowl of all kinds. To the initiate, duck hunting represents shotgun sport at its most suspenseful and most beautiful. Many of its adherents would pass up a week's gunning on any other game for one good flight of ducks swinging in to their decoys.

There are two major groups of ducks: the surface feeders, or dabblers, and the diving ducks. The most important part of duck identification is being able to tell one type from another so that you can set up your equipment to suit the particular birds that are flying. There are many ways that these birds can be identified once they are in the hand (I will go into that later) , but the important thing is to be able to recognize them when they are in the air and on the water.

SURFACE FEEDERS

We shall consider first the surface feeders, which include the mallards, black duck, gadwall, pintail, baldpate, shoveller, wood duck, green wing teal, blue wing teal, and the cinnamon teal. These ducks are called surface

5

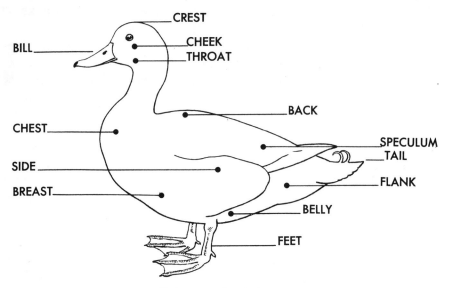

Main parts of a duck.

feeders because of their manner of feeding, at the surface on shallow sloughs, ponds, small lakes, and grain fields. They must learn to survive in rather close quarters with predators, and they rely on alertness and the quick get-away rather than on large expanses of open water to protect themselves from their enemies. When they launch themselves from the water, they rise directly upward as shown in the picture. The appearance of surface feeders on

FEEDING

RISING

the water and in the air differs considerably from the divers. Compared to divers, surface feeders have longer and more slender necks, longer bills, less chunky bodies, and slightly longer wings. The surface feeder's wings also have a slower beat, although the wing beat of both groups is more rapid than that of most other waterfowl. You will also find, especially among surface feeders, that the larger ducks beat their wings at a considerably slower rate than the very small ducks such as the teal. On the water, the surface feeders ride fairly high, with the tips of their tails turned upward; their heads are held a bit higher, except in resting poses, revealing a longer, more slender neck. It is even possible to make an intelligent guess as to the general grouping, at least in duck flocks flying at great distances from the viewer. The surface feeders usually fly in random bunches and strings that are constantly changing form, and only rarely in geometrically formed flocks. When flying in really large flocks, their formations resemble amorphous cloud shapes.

At close range there are many other ways by which we can tell the surface feeders from the divers. The fourth toe on the back of the leg, near the heel, is not lobed on the surface feeders, and the relative size of the foot is smaller. The proportions of the bill are longer and narrower; the speculum (the patch of color on the secondary wing feathers) is usually brightly colored; and the hen colorations have a mottled appearance.

Each of the surface-feeder species has its own identifying features. The following are some significant features of each species.

Mallard

Drake—Metallic green head, white-ringed neck, chestnut breast, gray stomach, black and white tail, yellow bill, iridescent blue wing speculum with white and black borders.

Hen—Mottled brown. blue wing speculum with white and black border, orange bill.

Black Duck

Both sexes similar—Mottled dark brown, purplish-blue wing speculum with black border, yellow to greenish bill, reddish-orange legs.

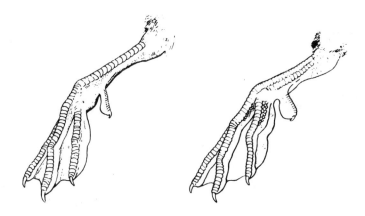

Comparison between foot of surface-feeding duck (left) and diving duck (right). Note that the diving duck's fourth toe on the back of the leg is lobed; the surface feeder's is not. The diving duck's foot is slightly larger than the surface feeder's.

Gadwall

Drake—Gray, brownish neck and head, black feather above and below grayish tail, white and black in wing speculum, brown patch at bend of wing, whitish belly, yellow feet, dark bill.

Hen—Body almost completely mottled brown, whitish belly, white and brown speculum, orange bill, yellow feet.

Pintail

Drake—Long, pointed tail, long, thin neck, brown head, with white stripe extending up sides, white throat and belly, white patch at rear of flank, bluish-gray feet and bill, bronze, violet, and green speculum.

Hen—Mottled brown; duller speculum than male, tail not long like drake's, bluish-gray feet and bill.

Baldpate or Widgeon

Drake—White on top of head, green band from eye to rear of head, pink breast, whitish belly, bright green wing speculum, white leading edge of wing, blue-gray feet and bill.

Hen—Grayish head, brownish back, tannish-red flanks and breast, white belly, black or dark brownish gray wing speculum, sometimes with spot of green, leading edge of wing more grayish than white, blue-gray feet and bill.

Shoveller

Drake—Huge, spoon-shaped, dark bill, green head, white breast and tail, russet-colored sides and belly, blue wing speculum, yellow eyes, orange feet.

Hen—Huge yellow or greenish spoon-shaped bill, mottled brown body, blue wing speculum, brown eyes, orange feet.

Wood Duck

Drake—Hooded crest on iridescent green and black-purplish head; thin curving lines on either side of head; white throat with white projections up sides of face. Bill has black tip, pinkish-white top, red sides, and yellow border above base. Breast is dark chestnut, sides are creamy buff with black and white lines separating them from the breast. Back is dark iridescence; speculum is metallic greenish blue, dull yellow feet.

Hen—Ashy brown head with glossy green crest, white spot around eye, white throat, brown-gray back, brownish breast and flanks; speculum is metallic greenish blue, feet are dull yellow.

Green-winged Teal

Both sexes—small size, rapid wing beat, darting flight.

Drake—Reddish-brown head with wide green band on sides, spotted buffy breast, white belly, grayish body, green speculum on wings with outer stripe of black, gray feet and bill.

Hen—Grayish-brown, lighter below, grayish feet and bill; same green speculum as male.

Blue-winged Teal

Both sexes—small size, rapid, erratic flight.

Drake—Bluish-black head with white crescent moon in front of each eye, rosy cinnamon breast, belly, and sides flecked with black, white patches on flanks of rump, chalky blue wing coverts (on top of leading edge), iridescent green speculum with blue next to body, blue-black bill.

Hen—Mottled-brown body, with buff head and neck, darker brown back, white patch forward of tail, dusky bill edged with yellow, yellowish legs.

Cinnamon Teal

Both sexes—small size, rapid, erratic flight.

Drake—Long, narrow, black bill, cinnamon-red head, neck, sides, and upper breast, darkening to blackish brown on crest, dusky brown back with lighter cinnamon scallops, green speculum wings with blue coverts like blue-winged teal, yellow or yellow-orange feet.

Hen—Looks like blue-winged hen; yellow or yellow-orange feet.

DIVERS

The diving ducks of the commonly hunted and edible game species include the canvasback, redhead, ruddyduck, lesser scaup, greater scaup, ring-necked duck, American goldeneye, Barrow's goldeneye, and bufflehead. Divers have contrasting sets of characteristics from surface feeders. On the water, these birds appear to float lower, owing in part to the outline of their tails, which slant down into the water. Their heads appear rounder, fuller, and closer to the body. Most of the divers can be spotted at a distance on the water by the flashing white or light gray sides and backs of the drakes. In the air, the divers appear bullet-fast, as they have an exceptionally fast and constant wing beat. Their bodies in flight appear heavy, almost round, owing in part to the bright white of their breasts; their necks and tails look stubbier than those of the surface feeders. In feeding, the divers seem to tuck their wings tightly against their bodies, jump almost completely out of the water, and submerge with a single arching movement of the neck and body. This action is so fast that the eye can follow it in impression only, rather than in detail.

In the manner of take-off, the divers can be readily distinguished from the surface feeders. The divers take a long, running start, and are half running,

FEEDING

RISING

half flying as they gradually rise from the surface of the water. The surface feeder, by contrast, can be completely airborne in a single jump and stroke of the wings, rising almost vertically. Flocks of divers are much more regularly formed than those of the surface feeders, and these are the ducks that we see in magnificent strings and V shapes in the fall. Canvasbacks are the most commonly viewed in such orderly formation.

In the hand, the divers can readily be identified by their broad, short bills. Exceptions are the canvasback, which has a long, sloping bill, and the golden-eyes and bufflehead which have short but rather narrow bills. The speculum on most divers is gray in contrast to the brilliantly colored speculums found on many of the surface feeders, and the feet are proportionately larger, with the hind toe lobed.

The following are some significant features of each of the diving species.

Canvasback
Both sexes—Long necks and bill, fly in formations, yellow or yellow-orange feet, black bill.

Drake—Reddish chestnut head and neck, black bill, brown breast and rump, whitish back, flanks, and belly.

Hen—Brownish breast and head, whitish belly, grayish-brown back.

Redhead
Both sexes—Rounder head, shorter neck than canvasback, grayish-blue bill and legs.

Drake—Red head and neck, blackish breast, gray back, wings, flanks, and tail, white breast.

Hen—Mottled brown body, yellowish brown head, darker brown back, white belly.

Ruddyduck
Drake—Brightly colored in summer, drab in winter. May have bright colors at start of hunting season but soon turns dull. Bright colors include gleaming back cap, white cheeks, sky-blue bill, chestnut red neck, chest and upper part of body, scaled silver and gray belly. In fall, bill turns gray, crown becomes blackish-brown, breast silver and gray, back brown, pale belly.

Hen—Dark, brownish-gray cap, neck, upper breast, back, wings, and tail, whitish undersides, bars of black on back and lower breast, white cheeks, gray feet, legs, and bill.

Greater Scaup (Bluebill)
Drake—Metallic green head, bluish-gray bill, dark brown neck and tail, whitish sides and belly, white speculum on wings.

Hen—Dark-brown head with whitish feather patch around grayish-blue bill, brownish neck; back and body are dark brown, belly is stained whitish, white wing speculum.

Lesser Scaup (Bluebill)

Both sexes—Have shorter white speculum ($\frac{1}{2}$ wing length) on wings than do greater scaup ($\frac{3}{4}$ wing length), smaller, dark-colored nail at tip of bill than greater scaup, otherwise hard to tell from greater scaup.

Drake—Often glossy purple rather than green head.

Ring-necked Duck

Drake—Glossy-purple head, black breast, dark, greenish-glossed back, gray flanks, white sides and belly; grayish bill with black tip separated from rest of bill by white ring; pale blue speculum on wing.

Hen—Mottled brown, white ring above eye and white line extending from this ring to back of head.

American Goldeneye (Common Goldeneye)

Drake—Glossy green, round head with circular patch below and in front of golden eyes; short neck, white breast, neck, flanks, and belly; back is dark gray hatched with white at sides; orange or yellow feet with dark webs; dark grayish bill; large white patch on wings.

Hen—Brown head, golden eye, dark grayish bill with a tip that turns yellow at breeding time; gray-white neck; lower breast and belly, scaled-gray sides and foreback; sooty rump and tail, white patch on wings is smaller than males; orange or yellow feet with dark webs.

Barrows' Goldeneye

Drake—Similar to American Goldeneye except head is glossy purple rather than green, white patch in front of and below eye is crescent-shaped rather than round.

Hen—Has shorter bill than American Goldeneye, otherwise similar.

Bufflehead

Both sexes—smallest diving duck; large head in relation to body.

Drake—Large, iridescent, black-purple head; large white patch behind and above the eye; black tail and back; rest of plumage is white including large upper-wing patch; dark bill.

Hen—Grayish-brown back and head, white spot on lower rear-quarter of head, light grayish-buff flanks with lighter belly below, dark bill.

Other diving species include such less desirable ducks as the various coots (scoters) and mergansers which are not widely sought because of their fishy taste. In addition, the oldsquaw, harlequin and common eider should be mentioned as ducks which are found primarily in the sea. Scoters are hunted off New England coasts; harlequins seldom go farther south than Long Island and Puget Sound and are found north to Alaska. Oldsquaws have essentially the same range, plus the Great Lakes. Common eiders are found only in the North Atlantic, with related forms in the Northwest and Alaska.

RANGE AND DISTRIBUTION

Ducks are found generally throughout the United States and Canada, and while admittedly some states are vastly superior to others for duck hunting, the prospect of reasonably good shooting presents itself within less than a day's drive of almost any place in North America. This perhaps accounts to a great extent for the tremendous popularity of the sport.

After examining the map showing the nesting and wintering grounds of the mallard and the lesser scaup one might falsely conclude that their distribution is much more general than it actually is. Certainly there are areas and, of course, many other species of waterfowl on almost every pothole. Toward the end of summer, when many of the smaller sloughs and potholes

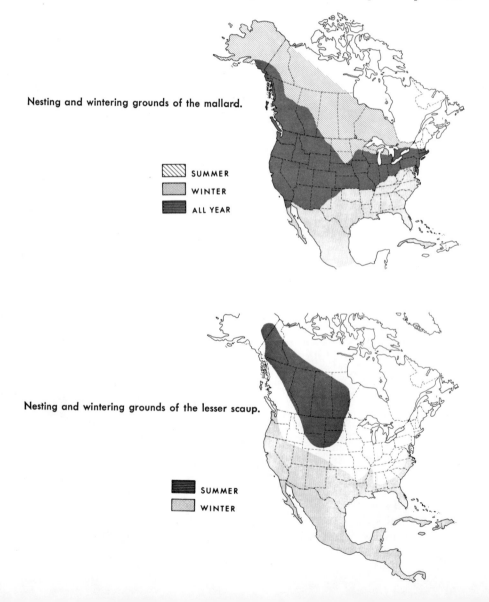

Nesting and wintering grounds of the mallard.

SUMMER
WINTER
ALL YEAR

Nesting and wintering grounds of the lesser scaup.

SUMMER
WINTER

dry up, the ducks congregate on the larger sloughs and lakes, often covering the entire surface. At this time, there is a constant stream of ducks going to and from the feeding fields on these waters. Such duck activity is limited to the more remote sections of the prairie states and Canadian provinces. Today, one must travel there, or to the wintering grounds, to see large concentrations of ducks anymore.

We see .by the map that the mallard's wintering grounds are at least as widespread as its nesting grounds. The tendency of the mallard to winter farther and farther in the North has been increasingly noticed. In winters of comparatively light snowfall, when ducks can feed in the grain-stubble fields, mallards have been known to winter as far north as central Minnesota, mostly on open spots in the Mississippi River, and on the Missouri River, below the Garrison Reservoir dam in North Dakota. This is surprising considering the fact that both of these areas are subject to long stretches of sub-zero temperatures throughout December, January, and February. Apparently it is not the cold that drives these birds south, but the decreasing availability of open water and food.

The lesser scaup or bluebill, is also an interesting duck, and continues to be a mainstay of the duck hunter's sport. This is not so much a result of its adaptability but, as can be seen on the map of its breeding and wintering grounds, of the fact that it breeds primarily in the far North. During dry years this duck will move steadily north until suitable water is found and in this way compensates for water conditions which substantially impair the reproduction of most species. The inability of the canvasback and the red-head to do the same (their natural breeding grounds are the shallow sloughs and potholes of the prairie region) has resulted in great decimation of their numbers during dry years. In the last few years, this has necessitated the total protection of these species. Both of these latter ducks, however, have been known to make remarkable comebacks in just a few wet years. The lesser scaup's wintering grounds, like the mallard's, are spread throughout all the southern border states, the eastern seaboard, the west coast, Mexico, and Central America, providing good shooting during migration in almost every state of the Union.

Traditionally, experts talk about four major migrational movements: the Pacific flyway, the Central flyway, the Mississippi flyway, and the Atlantic flyway. One must also take into account the many mergings and cross-movements these waterfowl make enroute to their wintering grounds. Groups within certain species, for unknown reasons, migrate almost cross-continentally, going from their nesting grounds in the prairie region across the north-central and northeastern part of the United States, to their wintering grounds on the eastern seaboard. These flyways fluctuate according to weather conditions and are not to be taken as exact representations of duck behavior. I recall one autumn in the Dakotas in the late 1950's when a severe drought pushed most of their ducks from the Central flyway over into Minnesota, providing some of the best flights that state had known in years. Ducks, unlike many geese, traditionally feed in each area along their migration route, as long as the weather and other relevant conditions allow.

NESTING AND REPRODUCTION

The nesting and reproductive habits of mallards and bluebills are fairly characteristic of other ducks. Mallards pair off very soon after arriving in the north from their wintering grounds. The pairing off is preceded by some very strenuous activity on the part of the competing drakes and the hen. The most commonly observed pre-mating antics are of the drakes swimming about and bobbing their heads on the water in front of the hens. Another common sight is two drakes pursuing a hen in flight. She leads them a merry chase, keeping up a constant quacking during the entire ritual, which goes on intermittently for several hours. Apparently, this is nature's way of selecting the strongest and fastest drake for breeding purposes. After pairing off, the drake and hen remain together until the eggs are laid. The drake then goes into communal bachelorhood with the other drakes, often remaining in this company through the moulting period and into migration.

The mallard builds its nest fairly close to the water's edge, usually in the heavy grass. The nest is constructed of dry grass, leaves, and down. The clutch consists of eight to twelve light-tan to greenish-blue eggs. All ducklings are very quick to adapt to their environment. The hen is very important during the first two months of the duckling's life, during which time it is unable to fly. Ducklings follow their mother around in a regimented line, scattering at her warning and reassembling at her call.

I had an interesting experience one summer day while walking through the woods with my Chesapeake retriever. We were walking down a path, when suddenly not ten yards before us a hen mallard and her brood appeared. At first she was not aware of our presence, but the dog spotted them and immediately took off at top speed. The old hen gave one loud quack, and her ducklings scattered back into the brush with alacrity. She then lured the dog down to the lake shore, about 100 yards away, and enticed him to swim after her a good quarter of a mile. Then she simply took off, flew back to the path in the woods, and called her brood with a series of short quacks. Her young quickly reappeared, and they went nonchalantly on their way. I am sure this has been happening between foxes and ducks for thousands of years —I wonder if the fox ever catches on.

Young ducks will take to the water almost as soon as they are hatched, but they do not secrete sufficient oil from their oil gland to remain waterproof. The hen must use the oil from her own gland to preen the ducklings or they would soon become waterlogged and die.

Mallards often breed more than once during the season, particularly if the first nesting is a failure. These late hatches are often just barely able to fly before freezing weather sets in, and occasionally they aren't. I saw a brood of downy ducklings in central Minnesota one year in the middle of September; their chances of survival were slim. Fortunately only a small percentage of the reproductive potential of any species survives, and the same is true of ducks.

The lesser scaup follow the breeding patterns of the redheads and canvasbacks. They prefer the marshes and sloughs of the prairie pothole country. They adapt more readily to drought than either of the previously mentioned species and, for this reason, are in more constant supply. The lesser scaup does not nest in clumps of rushes in the open water as do the canvasback and redhead, but prefers tall grassy areas along the edges of sloughs, often on the very edge of the water. This contrasts with most of the surface feeders who generally prefer to nest farther back from the water's edge, often constructing their nests well back in grassy pastures near sloughs or lakes.

The lesser scaup depends on attractions of voice and appearance to secure a mate, in contrast to the mallard, which relies on hot pursuit. The drake lesser scaup is a beautiful bird in his spring plumage. In his mating ritual he ruffles up his glossy black crest and puffs out his brilliant white sides, creating a dazzling display. Coupled with this show of elegance, the dapper scaup calls to unpaired hens in the area hoping to secure a mate.

The nest of this duck, like that of the mallard, as well as other ducks, is well lined with down, the purpose of which is to insulate the eggs during periods when the hen must be away feeding or on a diversionary excursion. The eggs number from six to twelve and are of tannish-olive hue. The lesser scaup is a late nesting duck. For this reason their young are most commonly seen late in the summer and frequently cannot fly until autumn is rather well advanced. As a breed, these ducks are extremely hardy, and do not fly south as long as there is any open water whatever. Their young can stand proportionably tougher conditions than some of their less hardy relatives.

One of the most puzzling things connected with the breeding pattern of all ducks is the homing instinct. Somehow, ducks are able to find their way back to almost precisely the spot at which they are hatched, and will set up housekeeping either close by or on a neighboring body of water. Exactly what mechanism enables these birds to return to their birthplace unerringly is not known, but it is an established fact. For this reason, it is possible to completely eradicate the productivity of an excellent piece of breeding water simply by killing all of the young and the breeding stock that would normally return to that area after wintering.

FEEDING PATTERNS AND HABITS

An understanding of ducks' feeding habits is necessary to successful hunting, as it enables you to look for ducks in the right places, and at the right time of day. Ducks have varied feeding patterns, even within a single species, depending on what kind of food is available, and what the duck's preferences are. Certain generalizations can, however, be made.

A blue wing teal, of the small surface-feeding ducks, stands at the edge of the shallow slough where he hopes to find food. *North Dakota Game and Fish Dept.*

Surface Feeders

The surface feeders, when feeding in the water, much prefer the shallows, where they can uproot tender shoots and tubers, and pick up seeds and crustaceans from the bottom, while remaining in the protection of slough cover. The characteristic feeding behavior of the surface feeder is either the tip-up, or the scoop, sometimes called the dabble. In the tip-up, the tail bobs jauntily out of the water while the duck submerges both head and breast to pick up food. In the scoop, the duck lowers its head and neck until the bill is just under the surface of the water, then lifts its head up a bit, while shaking it rapidly back and forth to sift the food out of the water.

16

Surface feeders thrive on a wide variety of foods, but they have their favorite morsels. Seeds from the tops of bullrushes comprise a major part of duck food in the prairie regions, where this plant is especially abundant, but along with this, they consume a great deal of other plant and animal matter. Wild rice is one of the favorite foods of waterfowl in general, but it is only found in a limited section of the country. For the most part, the big open-water lakes have little food of value or availability to surface feeders. Sometimes, however, these ducks will get up in the shallows of large lakes and find vegetable matter and small fish and other animal matter on which to feed. Swiftly moving rivers offer comparatively little to ducks of either group in the way of food. Rivers do provide the advantage, though, of open water much later in the season than other bodies of water in the North, and their sandy bars offer excellent gravelling and resting opportunities.

Most of the surface feeders, particularly the mallard and the pintail, do a great deal of feeding in the cut grain stubble after harvest, until the final freeze-up comes. These ducks feed on several different grains with relish, but have a particular fondness for corn, barley, and wheat. If a small grain field

A mallard drake in flight. His head and neck are thrust forward as his wings generate a constant and powerful motion. *North Dakota Game and Fish Dept.*

Mallards and pintails descend on prairie pothole country to feed. Hunters need only set up surface-feeding decoys on these small waters which never attract divers. *Texas Game and Fish Commission*

has been lightly burned over, and a fair amount of roasted grain is left, ducks consider it a real delicacy, and they feed on it ravenously. The advent of large-scale farming, and the use of mechanical harvesting devices, which leave large amounts of grain in the field, have had a great deal to do with the feeding habits of the surface ducks. There is little question but that grain farming supplies a large amount of feed for ducks in the late summer and fall, and the availability of this feed keeps ducks around much later in the fall.

Feeding hours vary greatly, depending on the weather, hunting pressure, and the time of year. When there is heavy hunting pressure, especially in the stubble fields of the prairie country, the surface feeders, will become almost nocturnal in their feeding habits, spending most of the daylight hours sitting on the large bodies of open water. This is especially true of mallards and pintails. If the weather becomes especially inclement, these ducks lose much of their caution, and feed in the grain fields during the day more readily. As a general rule, however, the hunter should not bank on much success in the stubble fields except at sunrise and sunset.

When ducks are on good feeding water they feed throughout the day, taking only intermittent rests, and basking in the sun. There is protection on the water, and for this reason ducks nowadays prefer to spend the bulk of their daylight hours on the sloughs and lakes. The tendency to feed throughout the day on the water has a substantial effect on hunting methods, as will be seen later.

Divers

The diving ducks, like the surface feeders, have a variety of feeding habits and foods. The most common feeding pattern of the divers is to raft up where the type of aquatic plant life they prefer is in abundance, and constantly dive to the bottom pulling up tender shoots and roots. Some surface

A vast concentration of pintails fills the sky in Colorado County, Texas. The rice fields of the area offer good feeding grounds. Open pits dug in the fields provide cover for the hunters. *Texas Game and Fish Commission.*

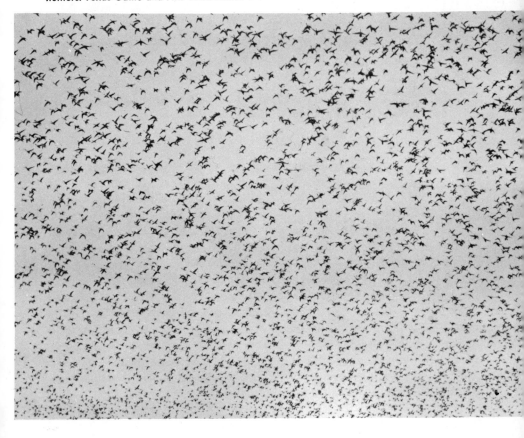

Many flocks of lesser scaup gather in Texas, one of their favorite wintering grounds. In the spring, these ducks fly far north to breed. *Texas Game and Fish Commission.*

feeders, notably the baldpate, like to sit among the divers as they feed and steal the food they pull up at every opportunity. Divers will plunge to considerable depths to obtain their favorite foods; most of these feed-beds are over 10 feet deep.

Divers also feed in the shallows, at times, though this is not their usual habitat. I have seen hundreds of bluebills feeding on minnows in only a couple of inches of water. The minnows had congregated near the shore, and were so thick you almost could walk on them. Ducks are supposed to taste very bad when they have been feeding on fish, but I have had many delicious meals of lesser scaup whose diet was nothing but minnows for better than a week. This is partly the result of immediate gutting and cooling of the birds in the icy lake water. Divers will also feed in the shallows on various crustaceans and other animal life.

As far as I have been able to tell, the divers follow no particular time schedule in their eating habits. They eat almost continuously. Unlike surface feeders, divers spend almost their whole lives in the water, except during nesting seasons. They are mostly occupied by feeding or flying around the big lakes they prefer in search of feed.

The feeding habits of all ducks become observable with the cold days of fall, when they gather in large flocks to migrate. Smaller groups within the large flocks, which may number in the thousands, often make minor feeding forays, and return to the main flock. One fall, I was hunting over a set of mallard decoys on a large rush-covered slough. A huge flock of mallards, about a quarter of a mile long, and fifty to a hundred yards wide, came over. They flew in column formation directly over the slough, paying no attention to my decoys, and funneled down into a barley field about one-half mile east of the slough. After the flock had been down about thirty minutes, groups of twenty-five to fifty birds began to take off and fly back to the slough water for a drink. These birds were full of grain and thirsty, and decoyed more beautifully than any ducks I have seen before or since.

LOCATING HUNTING AREAS

If you want to insure good shooting, and shooting with variety, familiarize yourself with the possibilities in your area, and obtain the necessary permissions, leases, or whatever else may be needed to hunt the places that look really good. The day is past when the hunter can go out on a Saturday morning and pick his hunting areas as he comes to them. Time presses during the hunting season, so looking for your locations at that time is profitless.

Sloughs

In looking for sloughs, I make it a point to keep two things in mind: (1) does the slough provide sufficient intermittent cover to allow the blinding of a boat; and (2) is the slough in a remote, out-of-the-way location, or is it readily visible from the road or highway? Many wonderful sloughs are no good for hunting simply because they are near a major thoroughfare. Slough systems are often the vestigal remains of ancient river beds which have turned into low, marshy areas. With this in mind, if you find a slough that is too near the road for good hunting beyond the opening day, you can penetrate back into the country either by foot, or by driving the back trails, and frequently find wonderful sloughs in the same chain. Detailed county maps are useful for this purpose and may reveal a great deal about the topography of your area that you don't know.

When looking the slough situation over, take note not only of the abundance of cover, but the type. Cattail, for example, will not attract nearly the number of ducks that bulrush will. If there are grain fields nearby, especially corn, this will add to the attractiveness of the slough, and may provide an opportunity to get in some field hunting as well as shooting on the slough itself. Access to sloughs is almost always through private property, and it goes without saying that permission to enter any of these areas is absolutely essential. I have always found the landowners to be much more agreeable if they are approached before the season opens. Constant harassment of owners during the season can understandably turn them against all hunters.

Lakes

Large lakes present a completely different situation than sloughs. I have hunted at many lakes, which have towns situated on two or three sides, and resorts or cabins around the rest of the shoreline, which were excellent duck lakes year after year. It seems that on the really large bodies of water, ducks are not very concerned about what goes on around the shore. The main thing to know about a large lake is whether or not a large number of ducks stop there every fall. Many lakes primarily attract divers; others, especially those with a large amount of marshy cover, attract mainly the surface feeders. I hasten to point out that one cannot find out how good a lake is merely by inquiring at the local filling station, although I must admit that I have resorted to that at times, myself. If you can, talk with dedicated hunting veterans in the area. Usually these men are willing to let the greenhorn know if an area is good or not, although they will rarely divulge the whereabouts of their favorite hunting spots. Attending the local sportsman club meetings (almost every small town has one of these) is probably the best way to meet hunters who are familiar with the area. Access to large lakes is increasingly possible by public landings. Many states are now legislating to purchase land for public access to many of the larger lakes. In looking for a duck-hunting lake, then, it is sufficient to know that it is a natural duck lake, that you can obtain access, and that there is sufficient intermittent cover to provide mallard shooting, or enough islands and points from which you can hunt divers.

Rivers

Rivers are much more difficult to evaluate than sloughs or lakes. The main problem in finding the best hunting spots on a river or stream is that so much of a river or stream is hidden from view. Practically the only way you can study a river for hunting is to walk along it. For this reason, rivers are very lightly hunted, especially if there is any other good water in the vicinity. Consequently, much excellent shooting is passed up every year. Most river situations do not offer much in the way of marshy cover; the current is often too swift to allow its growth. On the larger rivers, however, there are usually sand bars and islands on which scrub willow and other brushy vegetation grow, providing excellent cover for a blind.

I do not usually overlook a river as a possible duck-hunting location just because it is lightly hunted. If the river flows through good duck-hunting country, it will hold ducks, and will provide some shooting if you go about it right. Some of the least likely-looking places may provide excellent shooting along rivers. Naturally, the wide and shallow bar areas are nearly always good, as they provide gravel and good distances of open water. You should locate as many areas of this type as you can. Quiet, deep, woodland holes and backwaters can also be productive, mainly because of their remoteness.

When looking over slough, lake, and river situations in the preseason, it pays to keep an eye peeled on the surrounding terrain. A low lying area between two bodies of water, an isthmus, jutting points, or islands can offer excellent pass shooting. If you plan to do mostly pass shooting, it is a good idea to find the location of the major game reservations in your area, and the large lakes where ducks roost. Much pass shooting is done near these locations, although I have not found this method of hunting to be consistently productive. Most of the waterfowl comes off these bodies of water and flies at extreme altitudes, and good shooting can be counted on only in very stormy weather.

Fields

Good feed fields can be located with comparative ease, though the use of certain fields by ducks is not nearly as predictable as the use of certain waters, mainly because of the relative abundance of feed fields. Look for grain stubble, either wheat, barley, or corn, which have small potholes within their boundaries. If you can't find any of these, select fields close to large bodies of water where mallards and pintails are known to congregate. The bigger the field, the better, is a good rule to keep in mind, as ducks are very wary, and are reluctant to sit down next to buildings, woods, and so forth. Of course, permission from the landowners must be gained here, as elsewhere, and will be more readily granted to the preseason scout.

In general, when doing your preseason scouting, don't be misled by populations of local ducks. In the United States, throughout the northern duck-hatching states, blue-winged teal are very common. Many of these ducks may be spotted in August or September on the very small potholes and roadside ditches. Teal are excellent eating, and provide wonderful shotgunning sport, as they are among the trickiest ducks to hit. However, this species is known for its early migration (it is sometimes known as the 'summer duck'), and the first frost will often send them south. An area loaded with these ducks in September, may hold next to nothing on the opening day.

HUNTING METHODS

The most picturesque, and probably the most successful means of duck hunting today, is to be had while shooting over decoys. All species respond reasonably well to decoys and calling, and the chief species of both the surface feeding and diving categories, the mallard and the lesser scaup, are among the best decoying ducks.

Decoys

A good set of decoys, and knowing how and where to set them out, is mandatory when hunting large lakes. I have found that it pays to spend time analyzing the lake situation, evaluating wind, and spotting ducks and their movements, before setting out my decoys. Many hunters are so anxious to get out on the lake that they dash into the first clump of rushes, throw out all of their decoys, and find within an hour or so that they are in the wrong spot.

A good set of binoculars helps to spot ducks on the water and in the air. Once I have seen good numbers of ducks on the water, or good flights moving to an area that is obscured by cover, I load up the boat, and head for that area. I never worry about scaring the ducks out when I get there. In fact, I make a special point of doing this, because I know they will soon begin to return in small flocks of six to twelve, if no shots were taken. Frequently, ducks scared up in this manner will mill around the lake until the hunter has his decoys in, then return to the area and land.

If you see no ducks at all in the area the problem is quite different. The hunter must make a more intelligent analysis of wind direction than when he has seen ducks and has had simply to put his decoys out on the lee side of the open water there. The decoys must now be put out in a manner which anticipates the most probable movements of ducks during the day, and this requires knowledge of the kinds of ducks that will be moving. It is usually wise to select the lee side for your blind, as ducks dislike sitting in heavy waves. Moreover, decoys do not ride realistically in choppy water. Ducks of almost any species, however, will come in to the lake into the wind. If there are other hunters out you must make an effort to have the first set of decoys that oncoming ducks will approach, otherwise you may be hopelessly cut off, and though many birds are flying you may not get a shot all day. There are certain rules of etiquette that apply here, though, and you should never put your rig within two hundred yards in front of another man's blind. It is infuriating to spend time picking a good spot and laying out a spread of decoys, only to have another hunter come along and push his boat into the rushes one hundred yards in front of your location. This practically amounts to his shooting over your decoys.

Mallards are the most readily decoyed of all ducks, and also respond well to calling. In order to have good results on them one must put his decoys out in a natural manner, and in the correct position relative to his blind. I like to have the wind at my back and the decoys out in front as much as possible, although this does not give the hunter his easiest shots (duck alighting are most easily hit from the side) but it does hide the hunter and his boat from incoming waterfowl. The next best is the cross-wind setup, with the wind coming from left to right, if you are right handed, as this provides you with shots that allow easy swinging from right to left. As the diagrams for decoy sets for surface feeders show, the main bodies of the decoys are separated so that there is an open area of water in front of the blind. If this is arranged correctly, it will cause most of the ducks to land in the open spot in front of the boat. Do not put the decoys too closely together under any circumstances. This discourages ducks from landing in them and causes them to float un-naturally. If the set is not to the liking of surface feeders, especially mallards,

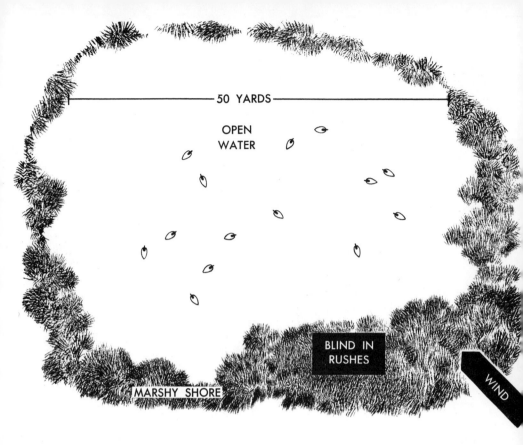

Small pothole set for mallards. Decoys are well scattered for visibility; the wind should be blowing from behind the blind.

pintails, and gadwall, they will often circle until they either see a flaw in the decoy spread, or spot the hunter, and fly away. If the decoys are too closely spaced, they may land far outside of the decoy spread and offer no opportunity for a shot.

Hunting divers on the large lakes differs from hunting surface feeders mainly because there are greater expanses of open water to cope with. It is extremely important to locate feeding ducks in this kind of shooting. If the lake is completely devoid of divers, I wouldn't go out at all, but would look for another lake to hunt. Once the ducks are spotted, one should proceed to the location quickly, and set up a shore, island, or point blind as close to the feeding grounds as possible. If the state laws allow it, a floating blind may be used. It is extremely effective when placed directly in the feeding area, or as close as the law will allow in terms of the maximum legal distance for such blinds from shore. If, by law, or some other circumstance, you are forced to situate your blind some distance from the feeding grounds, the old market hunter's pipe may be used to draw ducks within range. The divers will decoy well if your set is in an area which they are attracted to anyway, and they can be called with some success, though not as well as most surface

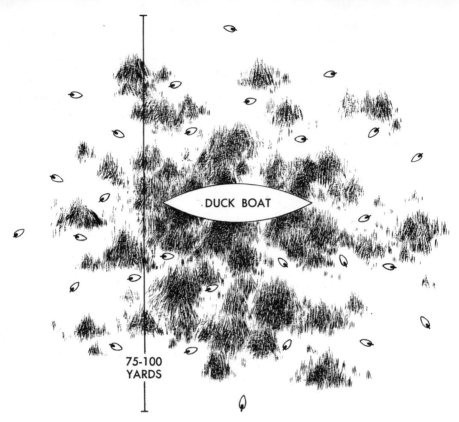

DUCK BOAT

75-100
YARDS

Marshy set for mallards with two to three-dozen decoys set in sparse slough grass. Decoys are spread in a feeding pattern around the boat, which is camouflaged in heavy cover. This is a good set for a calm day.

feeders can. They will frequently swing over the decoys just once and be gone, offering only a fleeting chance for a shot. Canvasback are especially noted for this. In all cases, the hunter should be careful not to place his nearest decoys so close that, in looking over the decoys, the ducks will also see the blind, and the farthest decoys should not be placed so far out, with the exception of various pipe set-ups, that they will cause ducks to land out of range.

Frequently the big water areas provide the opportunity to shoot divers and surface feeders at the same time. In a situation of this kind, I often set out my mallard and pintail decoys on one side of the blind, and the scaup, redhead, and canvasback blocks on the other. This usually works quite well, but at times the diving decoys seem to flare the surface feeders. When this happens, the situation can usually be remedied by moving the diver decoys out another twenty to thirty yards from the blind. I have no idea what causes ducks to flare from decoys of another species, but it does happen occasionally. However, I have had days when almost every flight of mallards that came in landed right in the midst of my canvasback and scaup decoys. Divers decoy best to their own species too, but if they are in a decoying mood, they will usually make a pass over a set of mallard and pintail decoys. I suggested spreading out the decoys in setting out for surface feeders, and this is even more true for divers. Divers come in at high speed, and land with a considerable skid. For this reason, they need more room to land, and will not come in to tightly grouped decoys. In setting out my diver decoys, I try to keep them about five yards apart.

Arranging the decoys on the river, though guided by the same principles used on the lake, is more difficult because of the current, arrangement of sand bars, and so forth. The swift water is a poor place to set decoys because they don't float naturally and tend to get washed downstream. The hunter should look for the quiet backwaters and pools and then situate his rig so that an adequate hide can be accomplished with reference to the wind. His decoys should be positioned so that ducks trading up and down the river will see them. Unlikely as it may seem, it is often productive to set up decoys for mallards among the shallow rocky riffles and rapids. Mallards like to perch on the rocks and sun themselves, pick gravel, and catch stream larva. Decoys can usually be set dry in this water, that is, they can be placed on rocks,

Decoy set for mallards around marshy island on windy day. Duck boat is camouflaged on marshy island; three-dozen decoys are set crosswind with open space between groups for landing ducks.

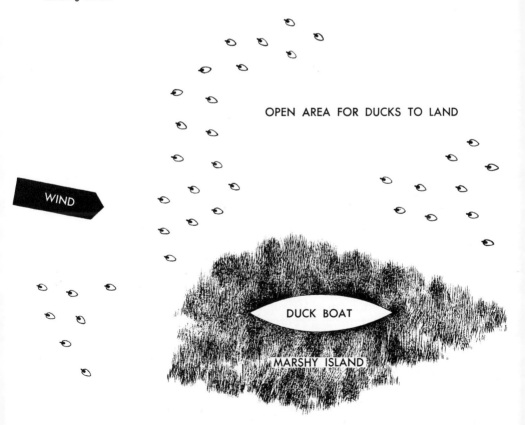

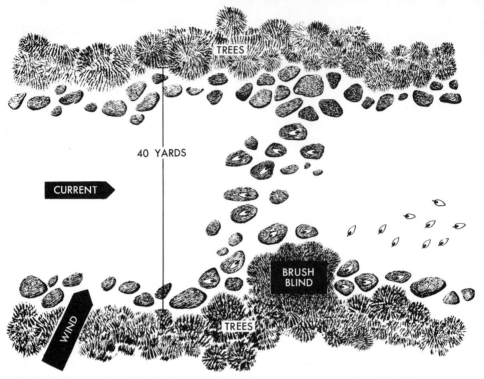

Rocky shallow set for mallards. About two-dozen decoys are set on rocks and in the water.

raised areas of gravel, or along the shore. Most ducks decoyed in this manner will come in pairs, singles, and small groups of four to six trading up and down the river. This makes for very exciting shooting and is also very colorful. A good retriever should be used in these locations or ducks knocked down in the current will quickly drift away.

In the small ponds and sloughs, I follow one basic rule in selecting my decoy site. I always try to place the decoys as near to the center of the water as the open patches will permit. When coming in to such water, ducks usually try to land as far from the shores as possible for safety. Use few decoys in the small sloughs; a large spread is not necessary, and may give the effect of overcrowded water. Usually six to twenty decoys will suffice in these places. The rules of keeping the wind at your back and the decoys out in front apply here as elsewhere. Hunting the small ponds, potholes, and sloughs provides shooting on surface feeders almost exclusively. There are occasions, however, when very stormy weather pushes divers off the large lakes, and onto more protected waters. There is no need to set up diving-duck decoys on these waters, though. When ducks are coming in to this kind of water, they will come in regardless of the kind of decoy used.

I have learned that weather makes little difference in decoy hunting on large waters. I have often had excellent shooting on days that have been sunny, warm, and only slightly breezy. Ignore the old saw about "bluebird" weather being no good for duck hunting. If the hunter equips himself properly, sets his decoys well, and can use the duck call to good advantage, he can have duck shooting in any weather.

Pass Shooting

The most demanding form of duck hunting so far as marksmanship is concerned is pass shooting. Many hunters regard pass shooting as the pinnacle of duck-hunting sport. Good passes are locations through which ducks naturally fly at a low altitude. Most of these are good year after year and will remain so as long as the local water conditions and duck populations remain about the same. Most pass shooting involves comparatively long-range shots, and this is where the big 10- and 12-gauge magnums come into play. One of the advantages of pass shooting is the low investment in equipment required. All the hunter needs is his gun, a pair of hip boots, a good retriever, and the knowledge of where to hunt.

Most good passes are heavily hunted throughout the season and many

Sand bar set on a river for mallards. About three-dozen decoys are deployed on the sand bar and the surrounding water, on the lee side of the blind.

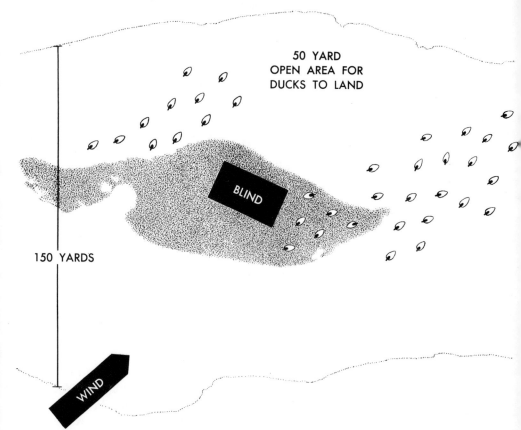

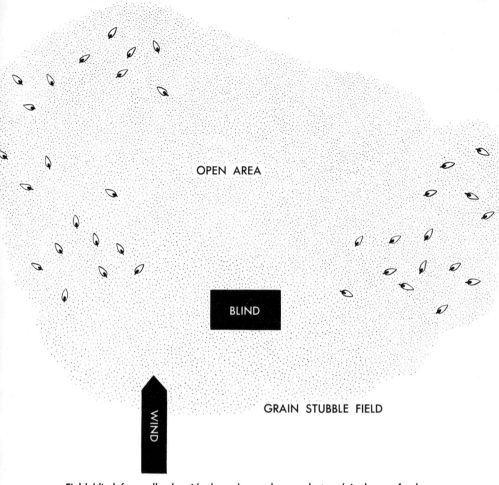

OPEN AREA

BLIND

WIND

GRAIN STUBBLE FIELD

Field blind for mallards with three-dozen decoys clustered in heavy feed areas.

are leased or otherwise made unavailable to the hunting public. The kinds of places to look for are the low strips of land between bodies of water, points, narrows, and low areas between sloughs or lakes, and grain-stubble fields. Sometimes passes can be located, especially in bad weather, by getting on a high hill near a good duck lake and examining the area through binoculars. If there is a really stiff wind, the ducks may be flying low off the lake into the wind, and one has only to get beneath their path of flight along the shore to have some excellent shooting.

Jump Shooting

Another form of duck hunting which appeals to the hunter who likes to keep on the move, and does not want to make a large investment in decoys, boats, and other equipment, is jump shooting. This is a rather broad area, and takes in any form of duck hunting which involves sneaking up on them, or taking them otherwise by surprise, and flushing and shooting them. One of the most effective means of jump shooting, and one which I frequently resort to if the action is slow over decoys, is to wade the shallow, grassy sloughs in the vicinity, or wade the lake shallows that have cover. Singles and pairs of mallards will usually sit tight in these situations until they are practically stepped on. This kind of shooting is at its best in the early afternoon when little else is doing.

Rivers can also be effectively jump-shot by floating downstream in a canoe, or small skiff, with another hunter, taking ducks unaware as you come around the bends, or by walking the shores of brushy small streams. A good retriever can be used as a flushing dog in walking the small streams, and may be necessary to rout tight-sitting ducks. When the opening day shooting scares most of the local ducks off the small sloughs, and the northern flights are not down yet, the remote areas of rivers and streams can be the best hunting areas. When floating rivers, it is a good idea to take turns at the oars, and let one hunter shoot at a time, in the interest of both safety and sport.

Another form of duck hunting, which may be called jump shooting, is when you sneak up on small potholes where you have seen ducks. The most common method employed in this kind of hunting, at least in the prairie regions, is to drive around the country back roads until ducks are spotted, then "belly up" on them, and try for a potshot. I don't have too high an opinion of this kind of hunting. When shots do present themselves, they are not very sporting, and it almost always involves more road pounding than hunting. But, as the old saying goes, "one man's meat is another man's poison."

Rocky shore set for bluebills feeding in shallows of a large lake. Decoys are spread out along the shore, some on rocks, to bring ducks in close. This set is used only when ducks have been seen feeding in these areas.

OPEN WATER

75 YARDS

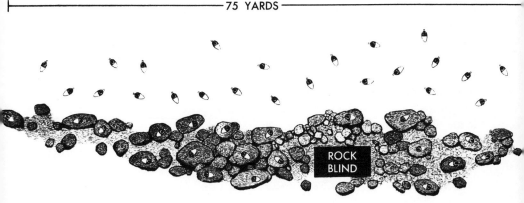

ROCK
BLIND

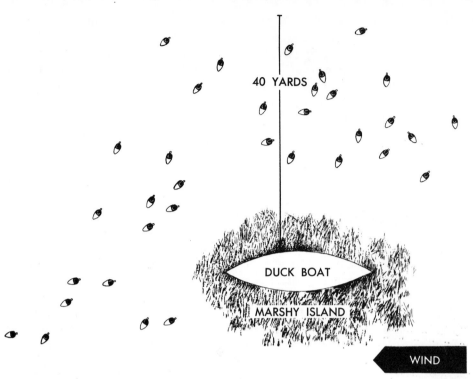

40 YARDS

DUCK BOAT

MARSHY ISLAND

WIND

Decoy set for bluebills used with a duck boat on open water. Three-dozen decoys are spread to allow landing space for the incoming ducks.

Field Shooting

Field shooting ducks is excellent sport, and is extensively practiced in the big grain-producing states, especially late in the season when much of the water area is frozen over. I have never had good luck field hunting for ducks, as I prefer shooting over decoys on the water to all other forms of the sport. Decoys can be used to good advantage in the grain stubble in conjunction with calling, or the hunter may situate himself in a field which he knows the ducks have been using, and simply wait it out. A field hunter must be an exceptionally skilled hider in order to fool ducks on these open expanses, unless he goes to the trouble of digging a pit, as goose hunters do. The usual technique if a pit is not used is to lie flat on the ground, and scatter a little straw or a camouflage net over the body for concealment. Unless a pit is used, the retriever should be used only after the hunt to seek out cripples. Otherwise, he will surely scare off most of the ducks. Like jump shooting and pass shooting, this kind of hunting is notable for its economy, and if your means are limited, and you live in an area where this sport is practiced successfully, it may be the one for you.

2

Geese

WILD GEESE are the big game of our waterfowl and are probably the most sought after of all our game birds. They are also one of our traditional game birds, having been hunted both for sport and food since the early days of our country. Though geese migrate through most states, many hunters have never had a shot at one of these magnificent birds. Geese fly very high and are extremely cautious about where they land to feed. They roost safely out of reach on large bodies of water, often on game refuges. The intelligence, wariness, size, and beauty of the wild goose has endowed it with a mystery that has long enchanted man. Enhancing this aura is the bird's plaintive honking call which sounds continuously as it migrates in the spring and fall.

Discussion of geese will include two basic groups: Canadas and the snows and blues. These geese comprise by far the greatest percentage shot in North American hunting.

CANADA GEESE

There are five subspecies of Canada goose, divided according to size. The Great Basin Canada goose, commonly known as the common Canadian goose, is the largest and, for its wonderful flavor, the most prized of all geese. This majestic bird weighs an average of 9 pounds and may weigh up to 10 pounds. There is a strain of the Great Basin goose, referred to as the giant Canada goose, which weighs up to 20 pounds, but so few of these are left that they form an unimportant part of the goose population. Like all Canada geese, the Great Basin goose has a gray body, blackish upper tail with white below, a black head and neck, and white cheek patches. This coloration makes the Canadas very distinctive and easily identified at a distance.

The Western Canada goose is second-largest. It is often referred to as the honker in its home range, which is limited to the region between Prince William Sound in Alaska and northern California. This goose seldom migrates and is found throughout its range all year round. The Western Canada goose is slightly smaller than the Great Basin goose, and is darker and the white cheek patches are often divided by a strip of black under the chin.

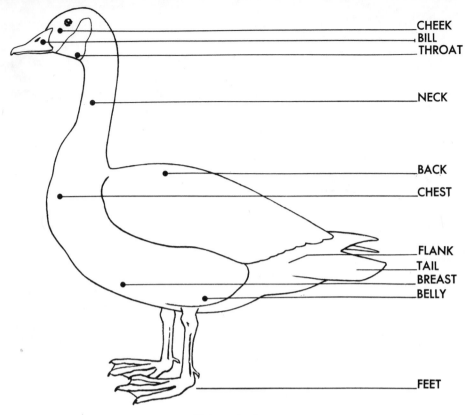

CHEEK
BILL
THROAT
NECK
BACK
CHEST
FLANK
TAIL
BREAST
BELLY
FEET

Main parts of a goose.

The lesser Canada goose is found only along the West Coast, the Gulf, and Mexico, and is the most abundant of all the western species. It weighs from 4 to 6 pounds. Richardsons' goose (Hutchins' goose), another subspecies of the Canadian goose, was for years confused with the lesser Canadian. It was discovered by Sir John Richardson on Hudson's Bay and named after a Mr. Hutchins. It seldom exceeds 6 pounds in weight. It winters on the northern shores of the Gulf of Mexico. The cackling goose is the smallest of the family. It is about the size of a mallard duck, weighing from 3 to 4 pounds. It is confined mainly to the West Coast. These birds are similar to the basin goose in color and other characteristics.

All of these geese are characterized by rather slow, steady wing-beats with the larger geese having the slower wing-beat. They have long necks in relationship to their size and have full, plump bodies. Geese have a different bill structure from ducks. They have longer legs which are situated more toward the center of the body, making them better adapted to walking on land.

BLUES AND SNOWS

In the opinion of some experts, blue geese and snow geese are color variants of the same species. Mr. Carl Strutz, one of the leading raisers of wild geese in the United States, has told me that he has found both snow and blue geese in the same clutch of eggs. Indeed, these birds look identical in every respect but color. They also breed in the same area, migrate together, feed together, and winter together. The same calls, decoys, and hunting methods work equally well on both snows and blues. Snow and blue geese both have pink feet and pink bills with a white tip, and black cutting edges.

The plumage of the snow goose is pure white with black wing tips, and a rusty tint on the head and face. The blue goose has a white head and neck with the same rusty tint as that of the snow goose, and a grayish-blue body with a light gray to white belly, and broad barring of dark and light feathers across the back. These geese fly in the V pattern characteristic of all geese, and can be readily identified by the alternate strips of dark and sparkling white in their flight line. Blues and snows have high-pitched voices and they call continuously in flight and on the ground.

RANGE AND DISTRIBUTION

The interbreeding of the snows and blues, and the difficulty in identifying the subspecies of the Canada geese, have made any positive limiting as to area, with regard to either wintering or breeding, a study for the ornithologist. Blue geese, while they are often described as primarily eastern birds, are found also in the West, and are also mixed with snows in the central United States. The snow goose, considered a western goose, is seen a great deal in the East; in fact, one of its major wintering areas is there. In addition, the nesting and wintering of geese are changing. The building of dam systems and game refuges has caused many geese to change their wintering grounds.

The Canada honker is easily recognized by his black head and neck set off by white cheek patches. They are the largest species of geese. *Texas Game and Fish Commission.*

For example, the Canada goose has practically deserted the Delta marshes of Louisiana as a result of the creation of attractive wintering grounds in the Cairo area of southern Illinois. Wisconsin is developing nesting grounds for Canada geese and is having some success.

OTHER GEESE

There are several lesser-known species of geese which ought to be mentioned. White-fronted geese, known as specklebellies, are primarily western birds, rare on the East Coast. They are recognized by their brownish heads and backs, with white feathers around the bill, and especially by their splotched black and white belly. They winter in central valleys of California, and along the coasts of Texas and Louisiana. A larger, darker, white-fronted goose known as the tule goose can also be found in one part of the Sacramento Valley. It breeds far up in the Arctic.

The emperor goose breeds and lives only along the Alaskan Coast with a few stragglers reaching Oregon and Washington. It is mottled gray with the head and back of the neck white. Brant (both American and black brant) are saltwater geese, seldom found away from the sea. The American variety winters along the Atlantic Coast from New Jersey south to North Carolina. Black brant is the Pacific Coast species. Both varieties are small, averaging 3 to 4 pounds. They have a black head and neck, and a white collar.

Ross' Goose is the smallest North American goose, no larger than a duck. It is found with snows, but is distinctly smaller, with a red, warty bill. It is now a threatened species.

Snow geese in flight. They are distinguished by the striking contrast between their snow-white bodies and black wing tips. *North Dakota Game and Fish Dept.*

Snow geese flying in formation with blue geese. Some authorities claim that both are of the same species, varying only in the color of their bodies. *North Dakota Game and Fish Dept.*

NESTING AND REPRODUCTION

From observations of geese in captivity, it has been found that a majority of them mate only once, forfeiting any reproductive activity in the event that their mate should die. Whether this is true in the wild is not known. The nests of most geese are located on a mound near a slough, or on an island in a slough or marshy lake. The nest is made of grass, and down is used to hold the egg temperature constant.

The Canada goose will sometimes use an abandoned eagle's nest in the trees. Some conservationists are taking advantage of this behavior and are building wooden platforms on which the geese are induced to nest. Goose eggs are large in proportion to the bird, white, and number from four to eight. The incubation period is twenty-two to twenty-four days in the smaller species, and twenty-eight to thirty days in the Canada geese. The goslings, like ducklings, are born with a downy covering, and are able to take the water almost at once.

The family life of geese is very interesting. Geese do not become independent nearly as soon as ducks, and owing to their size and awkward nature depend largely on the protection of adults for several months. Nature has devised a way of keeping the parents at home with the goslings. Shortly after nesting geese begin to moult, and they are unable to fly until new wing primaries grow back. During this period geese rely on their abilities to swim and hide to survive. Family groups stay together during migration, though they usually form larger flocks.

An experienced goosehunter knows that if the old leader goose is shot, the rest lose all caution and sense of direction and fly around in circles making easy marks. Geese, like ducks, have strong homing instincts, and tend to return to the same area in which they were hatched to build their own nests. However, conservationists have been able to induce captured geese to nest in a new area, with the result that the young return to reproduce there the following year.

FEEDING HABITS AND PATTERNS

The food of geese is composed almost entirely of vegetable matter. Although geese are equipped rather well for walking on land they do a good deal of feeding in the sloughs and lake shallows as well. Geese prefer many of the same aquatic plant foods as ducks, and feed heavily on seeds, roots, and the tender shoots they can pull up from the bottom. In their water feeding habits, they closely resemble the surface feeding ducks. They tip-up, and work the bottom for seeds, roots, and other edibles, much in the manner of the mallard. Geese do not usually feed in the very small sloughs that ducks inhabit, because they prefer the safety of large stretches of water between them and the shore. This limits their feeding habitat considerably, and so large numbers of geese congregate in one area of water that they have learned is safe. Like the surface feeding ducks, they must feed in shallow water, or

Canada geese enjoying the protection of the Gambill Goose Refuge near Paris, Texas. Such conservation ensures the continued life of the species. *Texas Game and Fish Commission.*

like the baldpates, feast on the leavings of wild celery and other plants that the divers pull up. Geese sometimes feed on crustaceans and other animal life in lakes and shallow sloughs, but this comprises a small portion of their diet, and is not thought to affect the flavor of their meat.

Grain stubbles, especially wheat, barley, and oats, with some corn, are among the favorite foods of the geese. They approach this food source in much the same way that ducks do, except that they will fly much greater distances to and from the fields. I have heard reports of geese flying thirty miles each way from the game reservations in North Dakota to a feeding location, and a fifteen mile flight is not at all unusual. All geese have great powers of flight, and though these distances seem extravagant, they are no more than a normal effort to the geese. Geese will feed a good deal closer to their water area if they can, but usually the fields near these areas are heavily hunted, and the geese quickly learn to avoid them.

It is interesting to watch a flock of geese examine a field before landing to feed. Unless there are a number of geese feeding there already, in which case they will often fly directly in, they will circle for a long time trying to detect a flaw or irregularity in the situation which might spell danger. Once they are satisfied that all is well, they will sit down, usually in the very center of the field. A sentry will then be posted to keep a constant vigil. If the sentry spots any sign of danger he will give the warning call, bringing the entire

The presence of many geese feeding in this rice stubble field spells safety to the flock circling overhead. Sentries are posted at the left. *Texas Game and Fish Commission.*

flock to immediate attention. For a moment before they take flight, they are utterly still.

Geese, unlike ducks, also have a habit of grazing. Grasses are among their favorite foods, and when the right grassy foods are available, they neglect other food for it. They enjoy many of the natural grasses, such as common blue grass, particularly in the spring when the shoots are young and tender. In general, however, they prefer the cultivated grasses of young grain. In the spring, geese feed on almost any small grain grass, such as rye, wheat, oats and barley. They sometimes do considerable damage to the crop. In the fall months of October and November, geese make heavy inroads on fields of winter wheat and rye, both of which are just about the right stage of development for their tastes.

LOCATING HUNTING AREAS

Finding good hunting areas for geese in advance of the hunting season is much more difficult than it is in duck hunting. The main thing to keep in mind, in scouting for goose-hunting spots, is to be sure to select *known* goose areas. Nothing could be less fruitful than to choose your goose hunting locations strictly on appearance. Many presumably beautiful goose hunting areas never attract a goose of any kind from one season to the next.

Except for game reservations, water areas for geese are remote in every sense of the word. Extremely large, grassy sloughs and shallow lakes, situated well back in the prairie pothole country of the West are generally good. These bodies of water are not easily found, and when they are, the hunter has problems of transporting decoys, boats, and other hunting gear. North and South Dakota are the chief states for pothole hunting.

Not to be overlooked as water locations for geese are the public shooting grounds on both East and West coasts. These grounds are carefully controlled both as to the number of birds shot and the number of hunters allowed. A well-developed program of this kind is now in operation in California. There are also some excellent commercial hunting grounds such as the flooded rice-paddies of California. Some of these areas are controlled by exclusive duck hunting clubs. Of these, some can be hunted without invitation by paying the daily rate.

The Klamath, Missouri, Platte, and Mississippi rivers are all famous for their goose hunting. If there is a goose hunting river in your area, it will take little checking to find out. Usually, the best areas along rivers are bought up or leased by duck and goose hunting clubs, where you must pay a substantial fee. Most of the good areas are wide, shallow stretches of water with low-lying islands and points on which pits and blinds can be constructed. If you look for areas on known goose rivers of this kind, you can probably discover some good stretches not leased or claimed by exclusive clubs. Usually, large numbers of ducks and geese congregate on these waters during the fall and fly off to feed on surrounding land areas.

Good pass shooting can frequently be had on grounds near large lakes and sloughs designated as state and federal game refuges, though the lakes themselves cannot be hunted. Pass shooting requires fairly rough weather, however, for the birds to come down low enough for a reasonable shot, and some field decoy shooting may be had in nearby grain fields. Waters of this kind can be located by calling your local game warden, or by writing the state game and fish department.

Fields of grain stubble, particularly winter wheat and winter rye, are the best places to find geese feeding during autumn. If you plan to hunt from pits with a large set of decoys, these are the areas you should find for your hunting. I have seen many flocks fly over miles of excellent wheat, barley, and corn stubble, to get to these succulent grasses. The problem here is to get permission to dig pits, and haul dirt from these newly planted fields. You can suggest to the farmer that you dig your pit before the crops are planted. If you make friends with the farmers in your area, and reimburse them for the loss of cropland and the inconvenience, you will probably obtain the permission you need.

You should of course collect as much information as you can about the

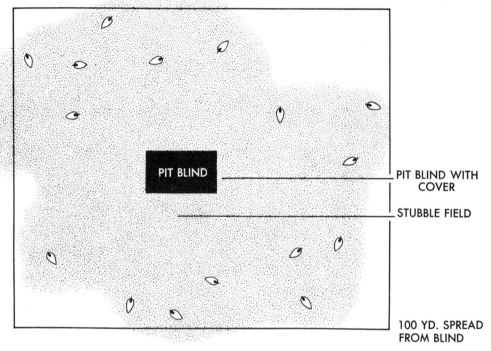

LOOKOUT GOOSE ON HIGH POINT
OF LAND NEAR FLOCK

PIT BLIND

PIT BLIND WITH
COVER

STUBBLE FIELD

100 YD. SPREAD
FROM BLIND

Decoy land spread for geese. Decoys are scattered in random feeding positions around the
blind (wind in any direction). Allow a few yards between decoys.

reputation of these fields as goose areas. Like ducks, geese are very fond of roasted grain, and if there are any burned off grain stubble fields in the area they are a good bet.

Two things must be kept uppermost in your mind while scouting for hunting fields. First, obtain permission for use of as many fields as you can; you will then be able to switch fields frequently, and will not "shoot out" any of them. Second, try to get fields with good histories as goose areas, the closer to goose waters the better. But do not overlook distant fields that are known to be productive or that have particularly choice feed.

HUNTING METHODS

The most successful, most sporting, and most popular way to hunt geese is over decoys. Goose decoys can be used with good results on both land and water. But in contrast to ducks, the land setup is usually the best. This is mainly because most migrating geese roost on the large game refuges. Once you have picked your fields you are ready to decide on a specific location for the day's hunt. If you have a number of fields to choose from go out the evening before you plan to hunt, find out which fields the geese have been frequenting, and set up your blind and decoys during the night. If you do this, you will then be ready to begin shooting at daybreak, which is the most productive time.

If you cannot find any signs of geese you will have to guess at which field to use. Knowing which fields geese have been flying over will help you to make an educated guess. When examining the fields, look for goose tracks and scattered goose dung. If large quantities of grass have been pulled up by birds, geese have been there and the field is a good prospect.

Decoy set for sand bar on a river. Decoys are arranged on sand bar around the blind and in the shallows. Wind can be from any direction.

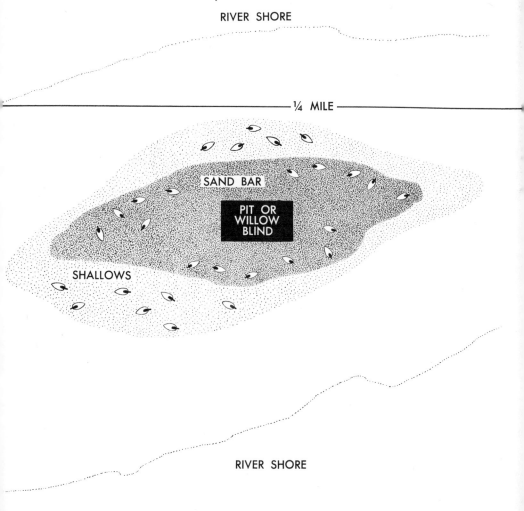

RIVER SHORE

¼ MILE

SAND BAR

PIT OR WILLOW BLIND

SHALLOWS

RIVER SHORE

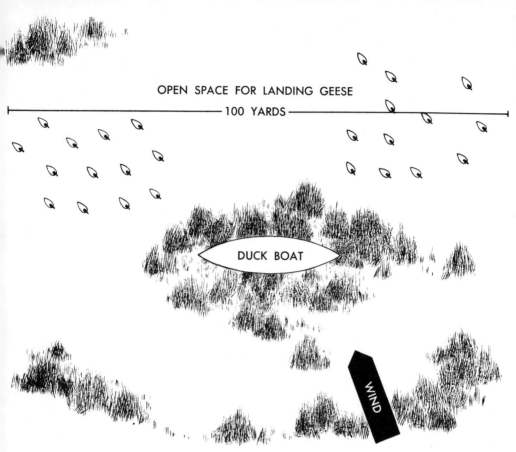

OPEN SPACE FOR LANDING GEESE
|———————— 100 YARDS ————————|

DUCK BOAT

WIND

Decoy set for geese on rushy island. Duck boat is camouflaged in the rushes and decoys are set on lee side of boat. Space between groups of decoys is landing area for incoming geese.

Decoys

In setting out the decoys be sure that your birds are spread in a natural feeding manner. A good share of your field decoys should have the feeder heads, some should have the resting heads, and a few should have the alert, upright head. If the decoys are widely spread they give the effect of a larger flock contentedly feeding. Decoys which are bunched together with their heads up look startled and convey a sense of unrest to incoming flocks. The full-bodied, silhouette, and nesting types each have their special advantages. (See Chap. 3)

If you do not have decoys, there are a number of inexpensive substitutes that can be used with success. Some of the best of these, for snows and blues, are the variations on paper decoys. Pure white paper bags can be purchased from any bakery for about one cent apiece. Blow them up by mouth, weight them with a stone at the opening, and place them in the field as decoys. A white paper napkin or piece of newspaper can be weighted with a rock or a handful of dirt. The flapping of the paper in the wind looks like a goose flapping its wings to other geese. Either the paper bag, the newspaper or napkin decoys can be used in conjunction with a stake head, which is a silhouette cut from cheap scrap lumber and painted to resemble a goose's head. The secret of successful goose hunting lies in the proper placement of decoys or decoy substitutes, good calling, and perfect concealment of the hunters.

When you first spot geese nearing the decoys, take cover immediately, and put your blind hatch in place. Calling can be kept up continuously as the flock approaches, but, if you are inexpert, stop calling when you think the flock has definitely decided to come in or else you are likely to frighten them away. Be patient as the geese approach; you have nothing to lose by waiting if the flock is still coming toward you. But if you jump up when they are still one hundred yards out, they will flare out of range. In goose hunting, as in duck hunting, I wait until they have their feet out and are ready to land, then stand up and shout at the flock. They rise almost vertically offer-

Combination set for ducks and geese. At least 100 yards should separate duck and goose decoys. A good set for either mallards or divers.

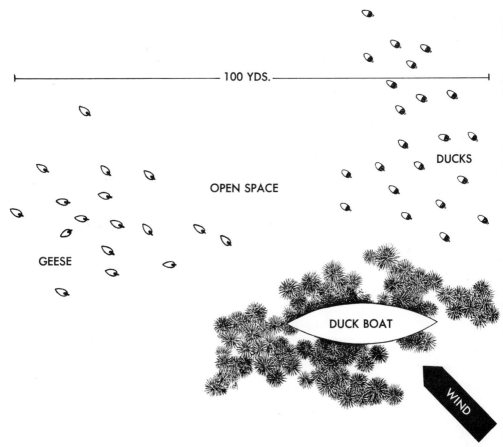

ing a good chance for a clean kill. There is nothing sportsmanlike about long-range shotgun work; it merely results in many misses and spoiled opportunities, not to mention the shameful waste of wounded, unretrieved game.

Decoy spreads that work with duck in lake and river shooting also work with geese. In river shooting, land decoys can also be used to good advantage on sand bars, reefs and islands. Geese like to be on dry land a good share of the time, and for this reason a combination of land and water decoys makes an inviting spread. Notice in the illustrations of goose decoy sets that the wind, as in duck hunting, is preferably at the back with the decoys out in front. I do not have nearly the faith in water locations for geese that I do in good feeding fields, but if you can find some good spots it is wonderful sport, and should not be passed up.

Stalking

Much hunting of geese today is done by variations on the stalking method. Some of this is conducted in a sporting manner, but much of it amounts to "meat huntin' " pure and simple, and lacks any semblance of real sport. Stalking geese amounts to little more than spotting the birds sitting on a shallow slough, lake shore, or field, and crawling up on them close enough for a shot. Rarely can this be done with any ease as geese are extremely wary. However, most locating of geese is done from a car, and often this involves chasing geese for miles until they sit down, then the hunters sneak up on them. Now this is not so bad, even though it amounts to a kind of harassment of the game, and tends to frighten them out of the area more quickly than other hunting methods. Often the use of a vehicle in goose hunting, however, degenerates into simply chasing flocks around the country, driving under them when they are low, and often firing at them from a moving vehicle. I have seen a pickup load of hunters speeding down the road at sixty miles an hour trying to keep under a tired flock, careen off into the ditch and across a ploughed field in hot pursuit. In much of the really good goose country, game wardens are so scarce that federal and state restrictions against this kind of hunting are impossible to enforce. I would rather spend the day with a good book than go at my hunting like that.

3

Boats, Blinds, Decoys and Calls

A GOOD portion of the joy and science of waterfowl hunting is the use and maintenance of special equipment. The hunter occasionally may take his share of ducks and geese using none of the equipment mentioned in this chapter, but the most successful sportsmen are those expert in the placement and concealment of their boat, the arrangement of decoys, and in the use of the call.

The recommendations given in this chapter are meant primarily for the dedicated hunters. If one buys the best boats and decoys, or constructs excellent ones himself, it is a considerable expense. However, the cost of this equipment is quickly forgotten, and the sport derived from its use more than compensates for the expense. It should also be noted that good equipment, treated with proper care, can well be a lifetime investment.

BOATS FOR WATERFOWL

A boat is one of the most useful pieces of equipment that the prospective waterfowl hunter can invest in. If I were to give up all other equipment, with the exception of a shotgun, of course, I believe I could do a fair job, at least on ducks, with nothing but a good boat. Many factors determine the type of boat for the hunter in a particular locale. Some of them are the safety aspects, the amount and type of gear to be carried, the kind of water, and the availability of natural concealment. Many hunters want an all-purpose boat, one that will serve for both fishing and hunting under a variety of conditions. Others, limiting their craft to a particular kind of use, may want a specialized model.

In considering the selection of a boat, you should keep in mind the most severe tasks to which the boat will be subjected. This will, of course, mean extra bulk and weight for slough and small lake hunting, but this is far less of an inconvenience, and much safer, than not having an adequate

47

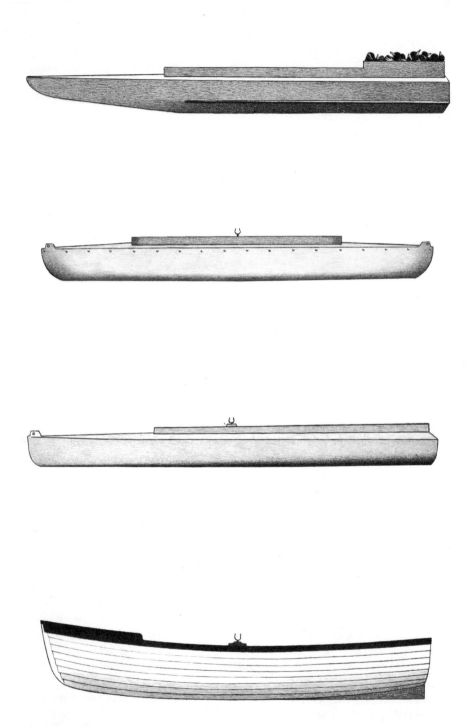

Types of duck boats (from top): Barnegat Bay sneak box; double-pointed aluminum boat; square-sterned fiberglass boat; lap-straked rowboat.

boat when you are on big water. The alternative to this, of course, is to have more than one boat.

Most duck and goose hunting done on the water is on sloughs and lake shallows. This kind of water is navigable in a small boat, and your main concern in selecting such a boat is shooting comfort and maneuverability in heavy cover. The number of gunners to shoot from the boat should never exceed two. You must also consider whether a dog will be used in the boat, and how much cargo is to be carried in the form of decoys, lunches, extra clothing, and other equipment. Therefore, even the shallowest, most protected waters are going to require a large boat if two men, a retriever, guns, ammunition, food and water, and fifty decoys are to be carried.

The hunter who likes to shoot alone and keep his gear light and portable, will do well to consider one of the small, double-pointed, decked duck boats

This hunter is equipped with an aluminum boat, useful in northern states where ice can damage plywood. Hip boots are necessary for marshland hunting. The dog is a black Labrador retriever. *Michigan Dept. of Conservation.*

A father-and-son team maneuver through heavy marshes in their homemade plywood duck boat. The push-pole is indispensable in most sloughs.

which are available in a variety of styles, materials, and prices, in lengths from 10 to 12 feet. These boats are light and easy to handle. The very narrow models of this type of boat are the easiest to pole through heavy cover and are more easily concealed in natural cover. However, they are not very stable, and a broadside shot with heavy loads may capsize the boat.

Even though the small slough boat is rarely subjected to rough water, it should be well decked and have a fairly high comb. This adds safety to the boat as the draft of a small boat leaves little distance between the water and the gunwale, and the slightest tilt would be enough to ship water without proper decking and combing. Also, decking is a handy platform for the hunter to use on which to climb in and out of the boat.

The shape of the boat, either round-bottomed, flat-bottomed, or v-bottomed, depends largely on the materials used. Most boats of a molded construction are of the round or semi-round variety. The chief advantage of this type is its superior seaworthiness. They have a fine ability to glide through rough water and cover with ease. However, a craft with a round bottom provides the least stable shooting platform of the three types. Some very good duck boats have a modified round bottom; the major portion of the bottom is flat, and the sides are curved sharply up, giving some of the advantages of both the round and the flat bottoms.

The color of the duck boat is important but little concrete advice can be given as to the specific hue it should be painted because of the wide variety of color in rushes and slough bottoms. I do not favor the solid colored duck boat myself, but rather a combination of colors found in the natural setting where I hunt. The color to use is one which closely resembles the color of the muddy bottom of the slough of lake which you hunt. Brilliant mustard and brownish orange camouflage paints are attractive to the hunter but are quite visible in the average slough.

After the duck boat is given two base coats of the dark slough bottom color, it should be painted all over with random streaks and blobs of color closely resembling that of the local foliage. Little care should be exercised in painting camouflage marks as the more randomly they are applied, the more the boat's outline will be obscured, and the less cover will be needed to hide it. Do not worry about spoiling the looks of your new boat; you may be the laughing stock as your boat sits garishly atop your car on Friday night, but on Saturday morning out on the slough, you will have the last laugh.

The equipment with which to move your small boat should be of special design also. Some boats come with good oars and a push-pole, many of them come without any, and with no instructions as to what should be obtained. Remember that a long pair of oars is unnecessary for a duck boat. In fact, short oars give you nearly as much speed, increased maneuverability, and the ability to row through narrow passages without shipping the oars. Six feet is usually an adequate length for duck boat oars, and I have seen five foot oars in use that did the job. A small canoe paddle is also very handy in any duck boat; a very small, light boat can often be propelled with only a paddle.

A push-pole is an indispensable part of the equipment, especially for pushing through the heavy reed growths that abound in most sloughs. The push-pole should be very long in order to provide good leverage and to allow the hunter to stand comfortably while poling through the rushes. Ten to fourteen feet is an ample length for the push-pole unless the slough is deeper. The pole should be made of ash, fir, or some other strong resilient wood. White pine bannister material, often sold for this purpose, is practically useless as it bends and breaks easily. A self-opening push-pole head should be attached to the end of the pole to keep it from constantly sticking in the mud.

Some hunters like to use an outboard motor even on smaller waters. Double-pointed boats can be fitted with a motor-mount with little trouble and expense.

In the northern tier of states the duck boat must be equipped to withstand the abuse of ice. Rarely does a season go by that the northern duck hunter does not have to break ice to get to his shooting spot early in No-

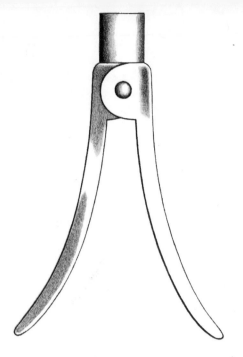

Push-pole head has a self-opening device to prevent it from sticking in the mud.

vember. Ice can destroy an all plywood boat in one season unless it is protected, and the best protection is fiberglass. This material can be quite easily applied to raw wood and is obtainable complete with instructions at almost any boating supply store. There is no need to worry about the fiberglass or aluminum boat. They become a bit scarred by the ice, but it is exceedingly unlikely that they will be punctured. I have been breaking ice up to one-half inch thick with an aluminum boat for the past seven years without any serious damage.

There are a number of places where the hunter may purchase a good new duck boat at a reasonable price. It is most economical to buy one of the unpainted plywood boats that are for sale in department stores, hardware stores, and boat stores before every season. The main things to be sure of are that the quality of the plywood is good, the frame is of hardwood, such as white oak, and that it is screwed or nailed and glued with waterproof glue. These boats are of the flatbottom variety and are pleasant and safe to shoot from. It is best if they are covered with fiberglass. This can often be purchased with the boat at a modest extra cost.

For large lakes, the demands in a duck boat are quite different. Safety, carrying capacity, and comfort are of prime importance and camouflage ease and maneuverability must be compromised to some extent. Some of the larger types of duck boat are also suitable for large waters if they have extra decking and combing, are at least 4 feet wide, and are 12 to 14 feet long. I prefer a good-sized rowboat for large water, as it will transport two hunters, a dog, and all of their equipment. A boat of this kind should be 14 to 16 feet long, and should have a beam of at least 4 feet. Although it is difficult to hide a boat of these dimensions, the added safety and comfort compensates for this flaw.

The color of the large-water boat can be considerably different from the small-water duck boat, especially if it is to be hidden along rocky shores or other locations lacking in dense vegetative cover. Muted shades of gray, olive, and tan are excellent colors for these boats, and I like a camouflage job similar to the broken color patterns of warship camouflage. If the boat is to be blinded in water similar to that of the sloughs, the smallboat colors should be applied.

You should use the most powerful motor recommended for your boat in large waters. This will enable you to get to your shooting site with a minimum of effort. It also will allow you to move quickly to another area as the movement of the birds indicates. Not of the least importance, a fast motor will get you safely off the water if an unexpected squall should come up. Some years ago, a number of duck hunters were frozen to death in their blinds during the great November storm on Lake Pepin in Minnesota, because they did not have enough power to get to shore when the weather became rough.

Boats for rivers are not radically different from other boats used in duck hunting. It is possible to use a canoe on small streams and in river jump shooting in which the two hunters alternate shooting and paddling at previously agreed upon intervals. Some extremely enjoyable and successful shooting may be had this way, if both parties have considerable experience in the safe handling of a canoe.

For many hunters on a limited budget, and with small storage space, I recommend a 12 to 14 foot square-stern rowboat, preferably of light and durable aluminum construction. This boat is adequate for any slough conditions, is very easily hidden, and if good judgment is used, is safe on most larger duck-hunting waters. There is a distinct advantage to having just one boat; if the hunter likes to explore, taking his hunting where he finds it, he will know that he has a good boat for all waters, and one which will also serve as a fine light fishing boat in the·bargain.

Boat blind constructed of quarter-inch metal rods placed in gunwale slots or specially drilled holes. Camouflage net is tied to rods and natural cover is laced to netting.

An effective boat blind is made by thoroughly covering a duck boat or flat boat with natural growth of the surrounding area.

BLINDS

A blind is any means by which the hunter, his boat, and equipment can be hidden from the view of incoming waterfowl, while blending with the natural surroundings. The hunter and his equipment should appear, insofar as possible, like an undisturbed part of the natural landscape. It is a good rule to use as much local material as possible in constructing your blind. Unless the hunter pays meticulous attention to the art of camouflage, he cannot hope for success. Our wildfowl are becoming smarter and more wary as they are hunted increasingly each year, and the hunter must gear himself to the difficulty of taking his game. Many of the old-timers claim that the only thing that will scare off ducks or geese is a movement of the hunter; this is no longer true. I have seen ducks flare from the silhouette of an empty boat improperly concealed, from a dog, from upset decoys, and from decoys of the wrong species. A hunter must be thoroughly hidden in his blind as well as motionless.

The prefabricated boat blind is one of the most convenient to use, and is also one of the best means of completely concealing boat and gunners from game. The best ones consist of either camouflage netting with a natural cover tied to it or a wooden frame to which the cover is attached by thin lathing. Both of these should be about 3 to 4 feet in height and should completely enclose the boat with the exception of one or two openings through which a retriever can slip. The prefabricated blind is completely portable and can move easily as the waterfowl moves. Its advantage over strictly natural cover is that the hunter can often "blind up" his boat in an exceptionally good feeding area of sparse cover where he otherwise could not hope to hide his boat.

The stake, or platform blind, is probably the most effective type of permanent blind for its particular location, though it lacks the virtue of portability. These blinds may be elaborately constructed and outfitted, incorporating many of the comforts of home: a gas or kerosene stove, luxurious seating arrangements, and so forth. Such a blind also has the advantage of becoming an accepted part of the landscape, and waterfowl will pay it little heed. If such a blind is overshot during the season, though, waterfowl will quickly get wise to it and avoid it. It is best to follow the example of the duck clubs and construct several such blinds on your shooting area and use them alternately. However, this arrangement is becoming less practical for the average sportsman as much of the good hunting water today is public, and legislation in most states permits the use of any blind on the water on a first come, first served basis.

Natural cover in the form of high rushes, tules, cattails, and so forth, make excellent blinds if they are sufficiently dense, and completely hide the boat. It must be close enough to the best shooting areas and decoy sites to make its use practical. As the season wears on, the weather and repeated use by hunters thins out the cover so that it no longer provides adequate concealment.

Permanent stake blind can be equipped with many comforts.

Deadwood combined with brush makes an effective blind.

Natural cover blind in clump of cattails.

Variations on the stake, or platform blind, the portable frame blind, and the natural-cover blind can be used on points, islands, and other situations close to water. Often there is a good chance in these locations of using existing cover for a blind. When constructing a blind in open situations, you should first survey the cover and color in the area and then try to make your blind look as much like an incidental clump of foliage as possible. For example, rushes can be cut from one area and be incorporated in a frame blind near by; rocks can be piled up in an already rocky location along a lakeshore; willows, sumac, and other brushy growth can be cut and stuck into the earth to provide concealment; white cloth can be stretched around a frame of four stakes if there is snow, or sheets of ice can be set up so as to give shelter and camouflage along an icy shore. These are just a few possibilities for the land blind near the water, and the resourceful hunter will learn to improvise with the most meager materials as he gains experience.

Finding a suitable blind in field hunting is a much greater problem than on most locations on or near the water because there is little natural cover left after harvest. The texture of the field is so uniform that the slightest irregularity is quickly noted by ducks. Without question the most effective blind used in field shooting is the pit. It is also the most difficult to construct. For the most effective pit blind you must haul away the dirt, since this is about the only way the tell-tale signs of your diggings can be avoided. When the time comes to replace the dirt, it must be tamped firmly back into place or an unsightly hump will remain there for some time. The pit blind can either be dug just deep enough to conceal one man in a lying position, or it can be an elaborate affair with wooden seats, kerosene stove, and other comforts comparable to the most elaborate platform blind. The pit blind

Rock blind on point in a lake arranged to conceal the hunter.

An adaptation of the stake blind, the tree blind is often used in the Gulf States.

has one outstanding fault—as does any permanent blind—it is immovable, and if it is not in a good location, it is of no value. The same reasoning applies to the pit blind as to the permanent water blind with regard to shooting from one location too often.

If pit blinds are used, several of them should be dug in various locations and each used no more than one day each week. Rotation of permanent blinds provides better shooting, but also tends to keep waterfowl in your area longer. If you wish to dig a number of pits, it is best to gain permission from the landowners well in advance of the season, and to dig as soon after harvest as possible. This gives your pit a chance to weather back into the landscape, becoming almost invisible. A simple hatch should be constructed of light, 1 by 2 pine and covered with a sparse application of straw or cornstalks. The hatch should be constructed with enough openings so that the hunters can watch incoming game with the hatch in place.

If there is a fair amount of straw, weeds, high stubble, or other debris

Fabric blind of white cloth stretched around four stakes is effective in snow.

Sheets of ice provide shelter and camouflage for the hunter stationed on an icy shore.

Pit blind in a field with the hatch open. These are difficult to construct because the dirt must be hauled away to leave a natural-looking field.

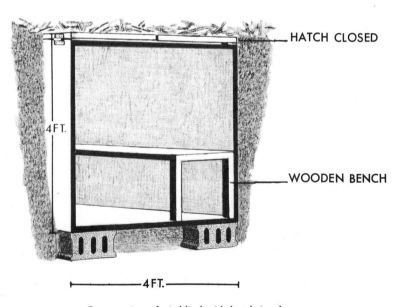

HATCH CLOSED

4 FT.

WOODEN BENCH

4 FT.

Cross-section of pit blind with hatch in place.

Natural-cover field blind made of clumps of grass.

A duck hunter making good use of natural-cover blind to wait for incoming waterfowl. Best use of such blinds can be made early in the season.

scattered around the field you intend to hunt, this can provide a good blind. The technique requires the hunter to lie down in the field between the stubble rows and to cover himself with some of the material. This type of blind is very effective, if done properly, but the gunner must remain absolutely motionless. Therefore he is not in a very good position to watch the birds or to rise for a shot when they come into range. A variation on the above method is using a piece of camouflage netting with scraps of straw and other cover tied to it as a cover for the entire body. My opinion of lying in a damp, cold field waiting for waterfowl to come in has never been very high, and I would much rather go to the trouble of making a more comfortable blind.

A novel kind of blind, and one which has been reported to be very effective—though it is illegal in some states—is the mirror blind. It is constructed simply by setting up four mirrors in a square, with the reflecting sides out. The mirrors must be large, approximately 4 feet square, in order to give enough room for a hunter. The theory behind this blind is that it reflects the surrounding terrain perfectly and thus becomes invisible itself.

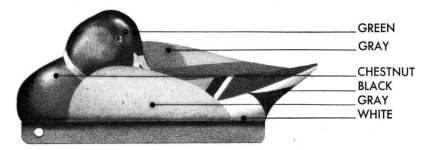

GREEN
GRAY

CHESTNUT
BLACK
GRAY
WHITE

Mallard male sleeping decoy.

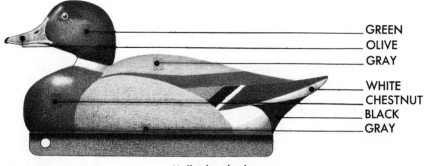

GREEN
OLIVE
GRAY

WHITE
CHESTNUT
BLACK
GRAY

Mallard male decoy.

DECOYS

The use of decoys in waterfowl hunting is of ancient origin. Archeologists have conclusive proof of their use by pre-Columbian American Indians. Attempting to bring birds into range by the use of decoys capitalizes on their social instincts. The social tendency becomes even more pronounced as winter approaches, food and water grows scarce, and the birds flock together to feed and prepare for migration. Their habit of gathering in larger and larger flocks as the weather worsens, leads many to believe that large numbers of decoys are not necessary early in the season. Although this idea may have some merit, I have always found that the larger the set, for any species, the greater the pulling power during even the earliest days of the season. This may be explained by the fact that the seasons in the northern states do not open until the first week or ten days of October, and, by this time, some rather considerable flocks have formed and have begun to migrate. Twenty to thirty years ago, the seasons opened in early September in the north, when the weather was still very summery, and the only ducks who had hinted at migration were the cold-sensitive blue-wing teal.

There are a great many different decoy materials, models, and styles on the market. All of them will do an acceptable job under particular conditions, but few of them serve the needs of the hunter in every phase of the sport. The weight, size, material, and floating properties determine the decoy you need for a specific job. Some of the very best decoy materials of the past are now so scarce as to make decoys constructed of them either unavailable or prohibitive in price. Some of these are: white cedar, white pine, hard Santa Marta balsa, and solid cork sheet. Granulated cork pressed in sheets is still available and not too expensive.

You may find a decoy maker who will fashion decoys from one of these materials, or you can carve them yourself. Either way it is expensive.

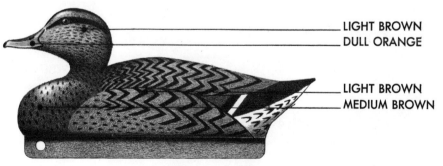

LIGHT BROWN
DULL ORANGE

LIGHT BROWN
MEDIUM BROWN

Mallard female decoy.

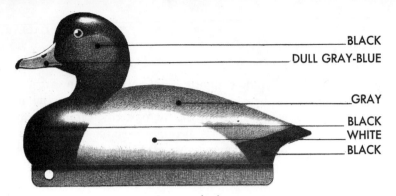

BLACK
DULL GRAY-BLUE

GRAY
BLACK
WHITE
BLACK

Scaup male decoy.

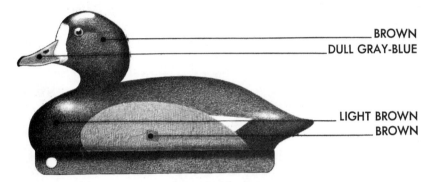

BROWN
DULL GRAY-BLUE

LIGHT BROWN
BROWN

Scaup female decoy.

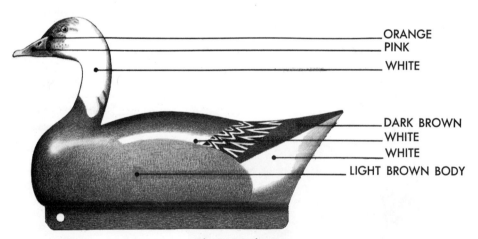

ORANGE
PINK
WHITE

DARK BROWN
WHITE
WHITE
LIGHT BROWN BODY

Blue goose decoy.

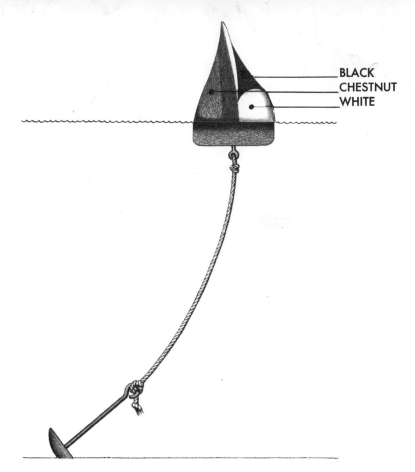

BLACK
CHESTNUT
WHITE

Feeder decoy and anchor.

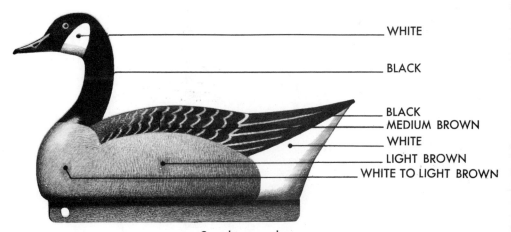

WHITE

BLACK

BLACK
MEDIUM BROWN
WHITE
LIGHT BROWN
WHITE TO LIGHT BROWN

Canada goose decoy.

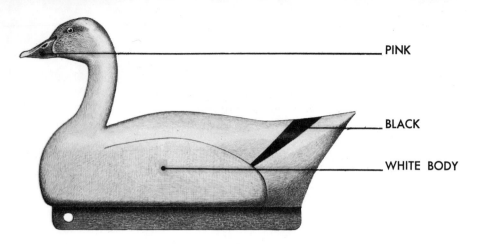

PINK

BLACK

WHITE BODY

Snow goose decoy.

Canada goose field decoy, can be made either full-bodied or in silhouette of plywood, mason-ite or sheet metal.

Canada goose field decoy, feeding position.

Canada goose field decoy, sleeping position.

Most hunters prefer a mass-produced decoy which has good design and a low price. The cheapest decoys are manufactured from pressed paper which has been impregnated with resin to make them waterproof. Molded tenite decoys are realistic looking but tend to become glossy with use. The best decoy I have seen is made of a hard-pressed styrofoam type of material, with a molded tenite head and a cast-in ballast weight. It is a very large decoy, easily seen from great distances, and is very lifelike in its design. The body

A pair of hunters setting out decoys. Using a push-pole, one hunter quietly guides the boat, while his companion spaces out the duck decoys.

of this decoy can become chipped with rough use, and if you want to improve its durability, give it a base coat with Luminall wall coating, a latex product for industrial use carried by most paint stores, and then repaint in decoy colors.

I have always preferred to make my own decoys, but this is not for everybody. In the first place, there is no great economy involved; it costs almost as much (just under $30 per dozen) to make large decoys from pressed cork

A hunter uses a duck call to bring in the birds. Mastery of the art of duck calling gives the hunter a decided advantage in the field. *North Dakota Game and Fish Dept.*

with white pine heads and plywood bottoms as it does to buy commercial models. Some sculptural ability is required, though this can be acquired through practice; and the whole process demands a lengthy and painstaking effort.

Decoys designed for use on land can be made of far less durable, lighter, and more portable materials than water decoys. Silhouettes made of pressed paper, plywood, Masonite, or sheet metal, are in extensive use, especially on geese. Some of these are of a semi-silhouette construction in heavy waxed cardboard of which the bottoms fold out and are held apart by a stick, giving a somewhat full-bodied effect. Some of these actually have the color pattern of the goose printed on the surface.

While silhouettes have been known to do a good job, most hunters of experience agree that the full-bodied field decoy is the best since they are visible from all angles. Full-bodied decoys of solid construction are extremely bulky though, and difficult to transport. There are, however, a number of concerns manufacturing a nesting field decoy in various goose patterns with detachable heads that are very good looking, and easily packed in by a couple of hunters. If one has the opportunity for good field shooting on ducks, the same decoys that are used on the water will serve very well.

DUCK AND GOOSE CALLS

The duck or goose call used skillfully can be one of the most effective parts of the hunter's equipment. The best way to learn waterfowl calling is to combine the advice and instruction of an expert caller and to listen to wild or semi-domesticated game birds. There are game farms, parks, zoos, and refuges all over the United States which have wild geese and ducks you can listen to and imitate. If you own a tape recorder, you can record various calls, play them back and practice them at home.

Calling wild geese is a much simpler task than duck calling because their calls have less variety. There are two basic pitches with regard to species: the low-pitched honk of the Great Basin Canada goose and the Western Canada goose, and the higher pitched cry of the blue, snow, white front, speckelbelly, and the lesser Canadas. Special calls are made for Canada geese.

Calling ducks is an involved and varied art. There are two basic kinds of calling: the quacking, chattering, and murmurs of the surface feeders; and the burrr-burrr-burrr of the diving ducks in three pitches, high for the scaup ducks, medium for the redheads, and low for the canvasbacks.

To call ducks successfully, one must first be able to identify the various species at considerable distances. Next, the caller must know the language of the particular duck he is trying to attract, giving the appropriate call at the correct range, and in the proper tone. Without a thorough knowledge of the habits and sounds made by waterfowl, the hunter should not try this method.

4

Bobwhite and Western Quail

THE QUAIL FAMILY

All quail in the United States belong to a biological order of birds known as gallinaceous (or henlike) birds. This order, which also includes the grouse, partridges, pheasants and turkeys, describes those birds which are terrestrial in habits and which have a food crop similar to the domestic chicken. Birds of the quail family have these characteristics and so are a part of this order.

The quail are the smallest of the gallinaceous birds however, and in the United States include six principle species, as follows:

Bobwhite quail (*Colinus virgianus*)
Valley or California quail (*Lophortyx californica*)
Gambel's quail (*Lophortyx gambelii*)
Scaled quail (*Callipepla squamata*)
Mearns's quail (*Cyrtonyx montezumae*)
Mountain quail (*Oreortyx picta*)

One other quail, the Coturnix quail (*Coturnix japonica*), has been imported from Japan but is not considered in this chapter because of its scarcity.

Of the six species discussed in this chapter, five are found only in the western or southwestern states and have been grouped together as "western quail." These include the valley or California, Gambel's, scaled, Mearns's, and mountain quail. Only one quail, the bobwhite, is found throughout a major part of the United States. Because of its widespread distribution, it is by far the most popular and the most widely hunted.

VALLEY OR CALIFORNIA QUAIL

Other common names for this quail are the blue quail, crested quail, topknot quail, valley partridge, and helmeted partridge. This quail has several distinguishing characteristics. It is small in size, averaging about

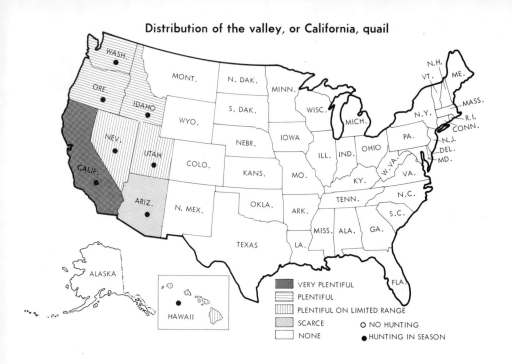

4 to 7 ounces, with lengths of 9 to 11 inches. It has a topknot or plume of feathers curving forward from the crown of the head. The over-all color of the male valley quail is olive-gray or bluish. The plume, throat, and part of the face are black. A white strip runs around the crown of the head and beneath the black throat. The top of the head is olive-brown. The upper breast, tail and back are bluish-gray; the belly is scaled in appearance except for a deep chestnut central patch. The wings and flanks are olive-brown.

The over-all appearance of the female is grayish-brown; the plume is brownish and shorter than on the male, the head is without the black and white markings, the throat is grayish, and the chestnut patch is absent from the breast.

As can be seen on the map, the valley quail is found only in seven states of the far West, and Hawaii. This bird can be hunted in four of these states In California, the bird ranks second only to doves in numbers harvested by hunters. It is the most common quail in Oregon, found virtually statewide. In all of the states where it is found, it most commonly lives along waterways, rivers and streams. In Idaho, for example, it is most often seen along the watercourses of the Snake River valley in the southern part of the state and along the lower Snake and Clearwater rivers in northern Idaho.

Males and females begin to pair off by late April and to separate from the covey and commence nesting in May. A nest is usually located in weeds or grass where a slight depression is formed. The depression is lined with dry grass or other plant material. From six to sixteen white or creamy eggs with brownish-orange or brownish-yellow speckled spots are laid. The eggs hatch after a period of twenty-three to twenty-four days of incubation by the female. The male maintains watch from a fence post, tree, or shrub during incubation and joins the female and brood after the eggs hatch. Chicks leave the nest as soon as they are dry. Feather development is rapid and the young can fly short distances within two weeks' time. Individual broods remain together throughout the summer, but begin to merge with other broods in the fall and form large coveys, sometimes with hundreds of birds in a covey.

As the name implies, valley quail occupy valleys, canyons and gulches, rather than the heights of hills. The home range of a covey is quite limited, usually being less than one-quarter of a mile in radius. These quail feed mainly on vegetable matter: clover, weed seeds, waste grain, berries, fruits, legumes, and sage. In addition, they feed some on insects, but only about 20 per cent of their diet is insects. Heavy snows limit the food supply of these quail so their numbers are seriously depleted by severe winters. The installation of "guzzlers" or underground watering devices has helped to increase the range of this quail in many parts of California.

Because of the habit of these birds of gathering in huge coveys in the fall, they will not lie well to dogs when so grouped. Particularly in sparse cover, the covey will run from cover to cover, sometimes for hundreds of yards, rather than fly. After flushing, however, individuals or groups of four or five birds lie well to a pointing dog. In fact, the birds will freeze in one spot for as long as two hours, making it difficult for dogs to find them, especially if the birds were thoroughly frightened when first flushed. Since the birds cannot be seen or flushed until practically stepped on, the use of a pointer is almost imperative. Even then, it is sometimes hard to get the birds to flush if they believe they are concealed. When they are flushed, the birds fly close to the ground, and on a downhill course, if possible. They may run a short distance after alighting, but once concealed, will stay put better than bobwhites, allowing the hunter with a good dog to find the singles scattered over a wide area. A comparatively slow dog with a very keen nose will find more singles than a fleet-footed animal that passes within yards without catching the scent under these dry, poor-scenting conditions.

GAMBEL'S QUAIL

Other common names for this quail are desert quail, Arizona quail, and redhead. This quail is similiar in size and general conformation to the valley quail. It has the forward-sloping, black topknot or plume on top of the head. The male is an over-all bluish-gray color with the same black throat underlined by white and the same white strip running around the crown of the head. The crown is a much more reddish-brown than on the valley quail; however, the color of the back is a slightly paler blue-gray on both sexes than the California quail. The male has mottled chestnut on the sides and flanks, with gray breast, sides striped with white, and a large black patch on a light belly. The female is much paler and does not have the distinct black patch on throat and forehead.

As shown on the map, Gambel's quail is found in nine states including

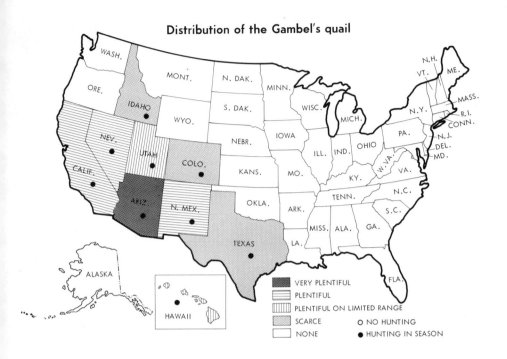

Distribution of the Gambel's quail

Hawaii. The bird is hunted in seven of these states. This quail prefers the more arid parts of the deserts and can maintain sizeable populations on the hot yucca and joshua vegetated expanses of southern Nevada, the brushy desert areas and irrigated agricultural regions in the lower elevations of southern Utah, in the dry, rocky regions of southwestern Colorado, and in river-bottom tangles of the junction of the Lemhe and Salmon rivers in Idaho. The installation of artificial water holes which catch and store rain water has increased its range in several states. Since populations in the desert are dependent upon rainfall and the subsequent development of vegetation, it's hard to pick the areas where this quail will be most plentiful.

Mating habits of the Gambel's quail are similar to the valley quail. Pairing normally takes place in March or April and by mid-April is at a peak. Each male selects a breeding territory and defends it against other males. Nests are usually placed in a lined hollow in desert scrub vegetation where concealment is good. An average of twelve eggs are laid over a twelve to fourteen day period. The hen, with occasional help from the male, incubates the eggs over a twenty-one to twenty-three day period. Both parents attend the young. The striped-back chicks are often flushed with their mother after several weeks.

Cover for these quail varies some depending upon the area. Along the Lemhi in Idaho, the quail are found in tight, impenetrable cover consisting of bunch grass, willow thickets, brush piles, brambles and vines where livestock cannot trample them. The mesquite areas along the Colorado River Valley offer excellent hunting in California.

74

The male valley, or California, quail is distinguished by the long plume, and the black and white markings on the head and throat. *Oregon Game Commission.*

Some of the feed taken by quail are seeds from filaree, milk vetch, cat's claw, blue bonnet, pigweed, wild sunflower, mesquite, dwarf locoweed, and other seeds and legumes. Cultivated grains and some green vegetation and insects are eaten when available. Family groups find food patches each day to feed, but return at night to heavy cover or briers for roosting protection.

Like valley quail, these birds are great runners and often hard to flush unless startled into flight. Once a covey is flushed, it scatters to all four points of the compass, making singles hard to mark and find. A good dog is a real help in pointing out these singles. Both setters and pointers can be used on the desert with good success. However, the hunter ought to take along a pair of pliers to pull out cactus spines from a limping dog's feet.

If you are unfortunate enough to be hunting these race-track runners on foot, you can charge from thicket to thicket of greasewood, mesquite, and so forth, trying to get the birds to fly before they run out the other side to the next thicket, or you can take it a little easier with a partner or two, try to surround the cover, and stomp and throw sticks into the thicket, as you close in on the birds, forcing them to fly. It sometimes takes several minutes to force the crafty old birds to take wing. They much prefer running from place to place in a large thicket or sneaking out at full speed to the next clump of brambles. Because of these habits, it is well for the hunter to get into good condition by running a mile daily over a period of time prior to hunting Gambel's quail.

SCALED QUAIL

Other common names are blue quail and cottontop. Cottontop gets its name from the pure white, cottony crest on top of its head. It is a larger quail than the bobwhite, averaging 11 inches in length and 7½ ounces in weight. There are two subspecies in the United States, one with a chestnut belly, the other with a gray-blue belly. Both sexes look alike and the over-all appearance is a somber bluish-gray tinted with dull brown. The breast and under part of the neck is buff, with scale-like markings on it and on the hind neck. The sides are brownish-gray, barred with white.

This quail is found in nine states mostly in the Southwest. It can be hunted in nine states. It lives in the arid sections of southwestern Kansas, in Cimarron county and in western portions of Texas, in the plains and foothills of southeastern Colorado, and other places. It is the most widely

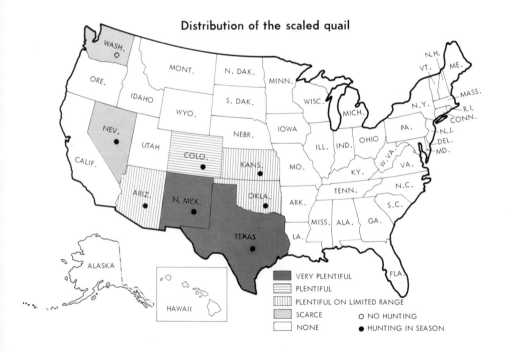

Distribution of the scaled quail

The scaled quail inhabits the desert country of the Southwest. It is hard to flush, preferring to sit tight or run when frightened. *Texas Fish and Wildlife Dept.*

distributed quail in Colorado and very plentiful in arid parts of New Mexico.

Because the scaled quail lives in dry, arid, desert country, its food is dry, and so it is dependent upon water sources. It often is found in brushy thickets adjoining a water supply such as a ranch windmill. Mesquite, cat's claw, cactus, spanish bayonet, chaparrall, greasewood, and various seedbearing grasses form cover or food for this bird.

Scaled quail begin to form large coveys in the fall and on into the winter. The chief problem in hunting them is to get them to fly. All quail like to run, but this quail is the fastest of them all, often running in excess of 15 miles per hour. A lone hunter trying to walk up a covey running ahead will find his birds have disappeared ahead or off to the sides. Therefore, it is better for several hunters to go together. Covey shooting is almost impossible, but when a covey is spotted, take off at full speed to try to flush them, then mark them down by small groups or singles. If sufficiently frightened, individual birds will occasionally sit very tight, so you have to beat the bush and thorns to force the birds out. Before it was outlawed in some states, these quail were hunted by gunners riding in trucks or on fenders, shooting the birds as they ran.

Most hunters laugh at trying to use a staunch pointer or setter. Coveys of the birds will not stay still under a dog's nose, but invariably run away. A good pointing dog is soon ruined with this type of hunting. Flushing dogs such as spaniels or retrievers, or almost worthless, nonstaunch pointers (but with good noses), are useful in running down the coveys and making them flush, but the dry, hot climate will wear down any good dog in short order. The cactus and various thorn bushes are also a real problem. However, a dog with a good nose, be he the pointing or flushing variety is very helpful in smelling out singles. Retrievers, of course, are very useful in finding and retrieving downed birds.

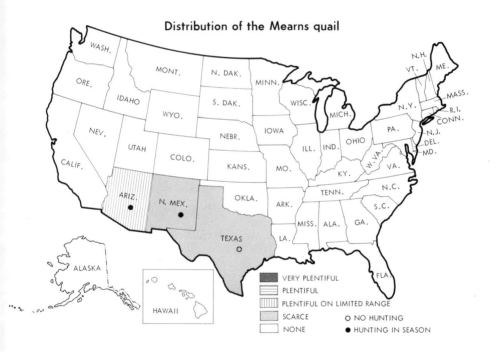

Distribution of the Mearns quail

MEARNS QUAIL

Other common names for this bird are clown quail, Montezuma quail (Mexico) or harlequin quail. No other quail is like it in appearance. The male has bold black-and-white stripes on each side of the face and heavy, white polka dots over dark-colored sides. The breast is patterned with a rich russet and velvety black. There is no crest or plume on the head; the female is a mottled brown with lighter buff belly and breast.

This bird is not well-known, primarily because of its scarcity; it is found only in the southern parts of three states, but is very common in Mexico. It will lie better to a dog than any other of the western quail; in fact, it is sometimes called the Mexican bobwhite for this reason. In good cover, whole coveys will sit tight under a pointer's nose and can frequently be approached to within a few feet. When the birds flush, they flush as a group, are very fast flyers and offer splendid targets. They fly only a short distance, however, and are easily marked down and relocated since they rarely run after alighting.

It is possible to hunt these birds without a dog, but a dogless hunter can pass close to them without even knowing they are there. A slow dog with a keen nose is preferred.

MOUNTAIN QUAIL

Other common names for this bird are painted quail, plumed quail, plumed partridge, coast quail, mountain partridge, blue quail, or pine quail.

This is by far the largest quail, sometimes weighing as much as a pound, but averaging about 9 ounces. The male and female are exactly alike; the general over-all color is blue gray. Its most distinguishing feature is the two long, narrow, upright black feathers which extend from the head, sometimes

Distribution of the mountain quail

Though the mountain quail is the largest of its species, its hard-to-reach habitat generally makes it less popular than other types among hunters. *Oregon Game Commission.*

curving slightly back over the body. The throat is a deep chestnut underlined with white, the breast is blue-gray; the back is olive-brown; the sides are rich chestnut with broad bars of black and white.

As the name implies, these quail are found in the mountain regions of five states along the Pacific coast; it is found along the watercourses in the central and southwestern parts of Idaho, and, in Nevada, in the Pine Forest Range of Humboldt County, the Virginia hills of Washoe, along the Sierras, the Wassuk range in Mineral, the White Mountains in Esmeralda, the Pine Nuts, and other places. In California, the birds are on the western slopes of the Sierras, the northwestern inner coastal ranges and from the Santa Lucia mountains of Monterey county south. In Oregon, mountain quail west of the Cascades are called coast quail; those east of the Cascades are called plumed quail. They are found in nearly every county of Oregon, but are most numerous in the Coast and Cascade ranges and in Malheur, Baker, and Wallowa counties in eastern Oregon.

Observers report that this quail is polygamous. Nesting takes place during

May and early June. The nest is a slight hollow lined with dry grass, leaves, or pine needles and is concealed under a log, bush, or fallen tree. From eight to fifteen creamy-buff, unmarked eggs are laid (the average is 10 or 11) and are incubated from twenty-three to twenty-four days. The chicks develop a small head plumelet during the first few days and are difficult to distinguish from adults at twelve weeks. Both male and female rear the brood.

Their diet consists of fruits (such as sumac, hackberry, black locust, huckleberry, wax berries and wintergreen berries), various grass and weed seeds, vegetable matter, and some insects. The birds can usually be found feeding close to dense cover. Since heavy protective cover is vital to the survival of these birds, during periods of heavy snow they will sometimes descend from the mountains to the river bottoms to seek out dense thickets where they will feed and huddle together for protection from the cold. The Clearwater and Potlatch rivers in Idaho offer this kind of winter protection. Individual broods of these birds do not group together in large, tight coveys, preferring instead to remain in individual coveys through the winter. Roosting takes place on both the ground and in trees; the birds make short migrations to lower altitudes in the winter.

One of the reasons this bird is not as popular as the valley or Gambel's quail is because of the rugged terrain where the mountain quail is hunted. It mostly inhabits remote ranges at 2,000 feet and above, and is seldom found in agricultural areas.

Like some other western quail, these birds are great runners (though not as fast as the scaled quail); they hate to flush, preferring instead to run uphill. The hunter, therefore, has to head them off by cutting off their uphill escape route. This is best accomplished by a group of hunters closing in from below and above.

When flushed, they fly wildly in all directions with a distinctive curving flight, offering some hard angling shots. The birds run for quite a distance after alighting which makes them hard to mark down. Once they find cover, however, they lie well to a pointing dog.

BOBWHITE QUAIL

In some parts of the country, particularly in the South, "quail," "partridge" or just "bird" means bobwhite quail, as though it is the only existing game bird. Certainly, there are more hunters of bobwhite quail than all other quail combined.

The bobwhite is a small bird, even for a quail, averaging around 9 inches in length and about 6 ounces in weight. It is not as brightly colored as other quail and is completely lacking in crest or head plume. The only way to distinguish the male from the female is by the color of the throat and eye stripe; the male has a white throat and a white line through the eye; the white throat is underscored with black. The female has a buff or yellowish-buff throat underscored with black and this same yellowish-buff color of stripe through the eye. This quail is mottled brown or chestnut color with some scattered

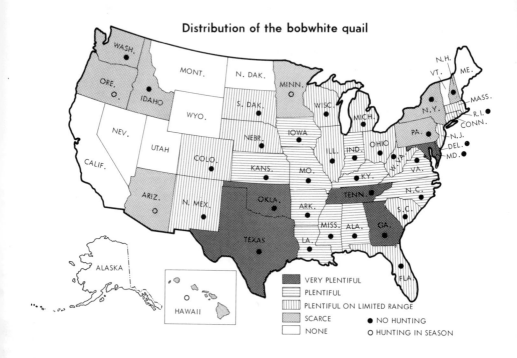

Distribution of the bobwhite quail

Legend:
- VERY PLENTIFUL
- PLENTIFUL
- PLENTIFUL ON LIMITED RANGE
- SCARCE
- NONE
- ● NO HUNTING
- ○ HUNTING IN SEASON

black markings and lighter shades of brown and white in stripes and speckles on the breast and belly. The tail is short and rounded.

The bobwhite quail is one of the most widely distributed of all of our upland game birds; it is found in 39 states and 37 of these allow hunting. Certainly, the bobwhite is most plentiful in the south-central and southeastern states. The hunter who wants the very best shooting ought to go to any one of the states where the quail is very plentiful as marked on the map. Also, in every state, particular areas contain larger populations than others. The state game and fish departments of any state will tell you the counties of maximum concentrations of quail.

The mating season of quail begins in early spring. Winter coveys begin to break up and the males begin whistling "bobwhite" from the tops of fence posts or other perches to attract mates. Since bobwhite are monogamous, as soon as a mate is attracted, a male becomes silent; those heard whistling during the summer are unmated. Because there are more cocks than hens in the wild, the males fight pugnaciously over the hens, but the brief skirmishes seldom are fatal.

In courting his mate, the puffed-out cock turns his head to show his white markings, and spreads his wings so that the tips drag the ground. Even though they try, bachelors are seldom able to lure hens away from their mates for paired birds are faithful and may even re-mate the next season.

The cock is very attentive to the hen throughout courtship, nesting, and incubation. He usually builds the nest by scratching a hollow in the ground with his feet and loosening the dirt with his bill. He then lines the hollow with grass or other material close at hand. Frequently the nest is built below heavy vegetation which forms a crude roof.

The female begins laying one egg a day until there are an average of thirteen or fourteen. The hen then sits on them during the incubation period of twenty-three days. Under conditions of extreme danger, or if something happens to the hen, the cock will take over the nest. But whichever bird sits on the nest, the other bird remains about twenty-five feet away, if possible. If flushed, the sitting quail uses the broken-wing trick to lure the enemy away.

About forty-eight hours before hatching, the peeping of the chick attracts predators. Of course, long droughts at any time may rot the eggs, floods may drown them out, and predators may rob the nests. If one nest is destroyed, however, the quail usually re-nests.

The chicks peck their way out of the shell using a hard horn or tooth which is on their soft beak. Although they can walk, run and feed themselves the first

The small bobwhite quail is the most hunted of all quail. This bird lies still when frightened, relying on camouflage for protection. *Tennessee Game and Fish Commission.*

Nest of bobwhite eggs lined with leaves. *Tennessee Game and Fish Commission.*

day hatched, the natal down is scant, so the mother broods them carefully for the first two weeks to keep them from wet and cold. After two weeks, however, the young birds can make weak flights.

The first true plumage begins to develop at about two weeks, but the process is not completed until about the second month. The birds are nearly full grown by four months. By the first fall, the birds have gathered together with other broods into coveys, roosting on the ground in a tight circle with tails to the center and heads outward, ready to flush in all directions. Coveys tend to stay together during the fall and winter.

Mortality rates among birds in the wild are very high. Depletions from predation, lack of food and cover, hunting, accidents, disease, weather, and other factors are enormous. H. G. Williamson, writing in a pamphlet under the sponsorship of the Oklahoma Wildlife Conservation Department, estimates that the annual turnover of bobwhite is approximately 85 per cent, and that the population is in direct proportion to available food and cover. Marsden and Baskett reported that in Missouri 82 per cent of a banded population of wild quail died each year. This is one reason why conservation departments urge hunters to harvest large numbers of birds each fall; excess birds in areas where food and cover are scarce will die anyhow. Winters of heavy snows and freezing rains are particularly disastrous; food supplies are covered, the birds are encrusted with frost or snow and die from over-exposure or starvation. Under the best conditions, less than 50 per cent of the fall populations survive the first winter. Accidents, predator and agricultural activities will take another 30 per cent during the nesting and rearing season.

Locating Hunting Areas

Generally, you are most likely to find quail in the food patches in early morning before nine o'clock Standard Time and in the afternoons from three o'clock to an hour before dark. However, weather conditions and predator disturbances affect the feeding periods. During rainy weather, coveys are more likely to visit food patches twice daily, since the wet vegetation discourages foraging in between times. Coveys living in areas where all their winter requirements for food are present on a small acreage of land usually visit food patches twice a day: once in the morning and again in the evening in clear weather. The length of time quail remain in the food patches depends upon

Bobwhite quail march along the edge of a grassy field, a favorite quail dwelling-place. Oklahoma Dept. of Wildlife Conservation.

the character and abundance of food and the protective qualities of the cover. Hungry birds feeding in soybeans can eat all they want in five minutes. Others take ten. Generally, however, the birds stay in the food patch about thirty minutes before flying away.

Also, an impending storm attracts coveys to food at any hour of the day, and at this time they remain longer than usual, perhaps even over two hours. The one exception is when it snows; under these conditions, coveys remain only long enough to fill themselves with food, generally five to ten minutes, then retire to their heavy brush cover.

Where do you find quail when they are not feeding? Generally, in brushy cover near more open food areas. Quail are notoriously birds of the edges, generally concentrating along the borders of some field strip or clearing. Of seventy-one coveys studied in a project area in Maryland, only three coveys spent most of their time in the forest. Ninety-six per cent of all of the coveys lived in brushy areas around field habitat. Swamps and dense forests are usually vacant. Furthermore, generally the first 50 to 100 feet of field borders have the greatest value to quail. This border strip provides escape cover; it is here that dusting, loafing, roosting, and nesting spots are available. The inside thirty acres even of a fifty-acre soybean field seldom attract birds, provided there is plenty of food available along the edges.

The movements of quail coveys are usually fairly limited, varying from ten to 300-acre areas. In general, the scarcer the food, such as in dense woods, the greater the area over which a covey ranges. Furthermore, there is often an overlapping of range of coveys. Especially at nesting time, individual members of coveys wander from the accustomed locality so that by the fall, any one covey is composed of various individuals of neighboring coveys.

The rest of the year, however, coveys stay together. You can be certain that coveys located by pre-season scouting will be in the general area when the season opens. Where food, roosting, and cover conditions are ideal, coveys usually only roam over about ten to fifty acres. However, quail living under forest conditions may occupy an area as long or wide as a mile, or about 300 acres in area. Quail always roost on the ground in the brushy thickets at night, feed in the food patches early and late afternoon and loaf and dust along cover and field edges the rest of the time. The best times to find them moving are when they move to and from the food patches early morning and move from cover to food to roost in late afternoon.

Hunting Methods

What is the best method to hunt quail? The most effective way is to use a good pointing dog. The bobwhite lies more readily to a pointing dog than any other game bird. Whenever in danger, this quail lies still, depending upon its camouflage for protection. This allows the hunter ample time to dismount (if on a car or horse) to cock his gun, take the safety off, and walk up on the covey to flush the birds. Then, once flushed, singles rarely run far from where they alight so that individuals can be carefully marked and hunted down. Generally, though, a hunter ought never to shoot more than a maximum of nine birds from a fifteen bird covey (about 60 per cent) as a conservation measure.

The denser the cover, the closer ranging your dog ought to be. If you hunt very dense cover with a fast, wide-ranging dog, he will get on point without your knowing it, tire of staying still, and may break to flush the birds himself. Such practices—if repeated—will ruin a good quail dog. Some hunters put a small bell on their dog to keep it within hearing distance.

The wise hunter will move from place to place, directing his dog to all likely patches of cover along fields, fence rows, and other edges. Most hunters travel on foot; if you have hunted over wide areas with a special jeep or truck rigged for dogs, hunters, maximum vision and mobility, you know how much walking it saves. Other hunters use horses. As for me, I have generally walked; I enjoy and need the walking.

Can you hunt quail without a dog? Yes, you can if you know where and when to hunt, but you are missing half the sport. It is best for the lone hunter to find small brush and food patches adjacent to open areas. Fence rows are excellent places for a single hunter to cover. If with a partner or two, try to surround slightly large patches of cover and come in from all angles. It's difficult for one hunter alone to flush the birds. Then mark singles carefully and you will have good shooting. It is well to remember too that birds flushed in the open head for the nearest cover. Sometimes a man stationed at the likely point of exit will be able to get off a fast shot or two.

Another method for a group of hunters is to line up about 20 or 30 feet abreast and walk the fields and edges trying to scare up coveys. It is not easy to flush the birds, but it can be done, especially if you walk erratically to encourage the birds to flush.

A flushed covey explodes fast and in all directions; the hardest task is for the hunter to wait until the birds rise, even off and fly straight away, before shooting. The hunter needs to keep his eye on one bird only and try to hit it. Never try to shoot the whole covey.

Quail hunting is not easy. A study of hunter success in North Carolina during a recent year revealed that the average hunter made about five trips per season, shot sixteen birds for an average kill of about two birds per trip.

5

Mourning Doves

OF ALL game birds in the United States mourning doves (*Fenaidura macroura*) provide the most difficult targets for the shotgunner. For this reason, some consider doves the most sport, though they do provide a tasty, if small, meal. Doves have been prized the world over for sport and food for many centuries. In North America, they have been overlooked until recent times, because of the abundance of larger and equally delicious game birds.

Many states consider the mourning dove a song bird and include it among the protected species. The coo-cooing of doves is certainly beautiful to hear, but moderate hunting pressure has little if any effect on the nesting population. For these reasons, I feel that the mourning dove should serve a dual purpose: to beautify the world with its song, and to provide sport for the gunner.

IDENTIFICATION

The mourning dove is a small, fawn-gray, pigeonlike bird measuring about 12½ inches in length, and weighing about 6 ounces. The belly shades to a lighter pinkish-fawn, and the tail and wings are barred or spotted with black. In flight, the dove has a powerful, quick wingbeat which gives it exceptional maneuverability and speed. The male and female are roughly the same in appearance, but the male is brighter and has more distinct coloration. In particular, the male has a more pronounced black spot on each side of the head behind the eyes than the female. In flight, it is practically impossible to distinguish between the sexes. The mourning dove has a small delicate head set on a gracefully tapered neck; a full, oval-shaped body; short, rather pointed wings; and a long, somewhat pointed tail. In the hand, the young birds can be distinguished from the older birds by a white rim around the edges of the wing shoulder feathers. This turns to solid gray in the adults. Game biologists use this information to study age ratios and annual reproduction.

The mourning dove resembles the pigeon and is distinguished by its long pointed tail. It is well known for its cooing song and is, in fact, protected as a song bird in many states. *Oklahoma Dept. of Wildlife Conservation.*

RANGE AND DISTRIBUTION

The mourning dove is found in 49 states including Alaska, and hunted in 32. It breeds in every state except Alaska and Hawaii. It is also found in Canada, except the far North.

Mourning doves are migratory birds, and with the first chill days of autumn they gather in flocks and fly South. The wintering range of the mourning dove runs from southern Oregon, southern Colorado, northern Ohio, and North Carolina, south to Panama. Generally, the cold winters of the central states preclude its presence there from December through March, but in a mild winter, it may occasionally be seen.

NESTING AND REPRODUCTION

Doves prefer woods, thickets and small grain fields, such as are found in most parts of the United States. They build their nests almost entirely in scrubby trees at the edge of clearings, and prefer pine, no doubt because of the excellent protection trees of this type afford. They build their nests in deciduous trees, bushes, and thickets. The mourning dove does not rely on altitude as a means of protection, and their nests can be found in branches only a few feet from the ground. Occasionally, doves use empty nests of other birds. The nest is rather loosely constructed of twigs and straw, and is of modest size, no larger than it must be to hold a pair of eggs.

The familiar *coo-coo* of the mourning dove is the mating call of the male.

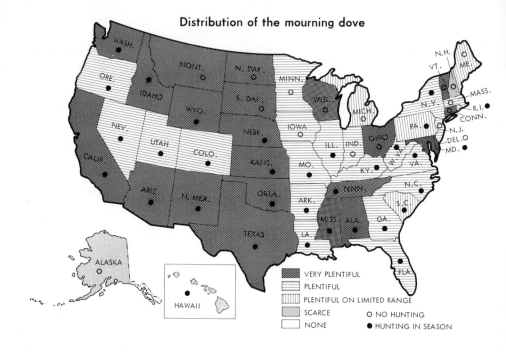

Distribution of the mourning dove

VERY PLENTIFUL
PLENTIFUL
PLENTIFUL ON LIMITED RANGE
SCARCE   O NO HUNTING
NONE   ● HUNTING IN SEASON

Since their mating activity goes on throughout the summer and often into September, the call can be heard almost anytime from spring until fall. Throughout most of the states, however, the bulk of the nesting is done in April, May, June, and July. The male and female build the nest cooperatively, and both participate in rearing their young.

The clutch of the mourning dove is small, almost always two eggs and occasionally only one, but they make up for this by nesting several times during the summer. Mourning doves nest an average of three times each summer, though some have been observed to nest as many as six times. The incubation period is only fourteen days, and the complete cycle of nest building, egg-laying, hatching, and rearing of the young to fledgling age, takes only a month. The fledgling doves stay in the area of the nest only a week or two, receiving some care from the parents, and strengthening their wings. They next join other young in flocks in nearby fields until migration time.

From the time the young doves are hatched until they are ready to fly, they feed on regurgitated seeds mixed with the digestive fluids of either parent. Natural predation, hunting, and other factors account for the rather high mortality rate in doves, as it does in other birds; the number left after a normal season is about equal to the number of nesting birds from the previous season. Improved or destroyed habitat, weather conditions and food availability can change this picture for better or worse. Most game authorities feel that hunting pressure, as it is legislated today, has little effect on the population of these birds.

FEEDING PATTERNS AND HABITS

The main diet of the mourning dove is seeds. Doves eat a great variety of seeds, including waste grain after harvest, weed seeds of all kinds, and seeds of the various grasses. I have also seen them feeding on wild fruits, such as grapes, currants, gooseberries, and choke cherries. Doves feed sporadically throughout the day, but prefer feeding in the late afternoon. When eating, the small birds crouch close to the ground in an effort to hide from the searching eyes of the hawk. ,

Mourning doves roost in the evening, relying on the protection of the heaviest thickets. In almost any area where there are many mourning doves, one can go to brush-lined streams, groves, and other patches of heavy timber and brush at about sundown, and see large numbers of doves flying in to roost. This is especially true in late summer and fall, just before migration, when they concentrate in these areas in large numbers. A gravel pit with water

The mourning dove nests at the edge of woods and thickets and relies more on natural camouflage than altitude for safety. *North Dakota Game and Fish Dept.*

standing in it is an excellent place to observe doves in the morning. Frequently, after feeding and roosting intermittently during the day, these birds return to their watering and gravelling sites late in the afternoon, before roosting. Doves can often be seen taking gravel along the edges of dirt roads both early in the morning and late in the afternoon. In these habits, they resemble many of our upland game birds, notably the pheasant, grouse, partridge, and other gallinaceous fowl.

The mourning dove has a strong flocking instinct in the fall before migration. As autumn progresses, doves can be seen in increasingly large groups while feeding, roosting, watering and picking gravel. I have seen several hundred doves feeding at once in a rather small area of grain stubble in the fall, and have also seen some tremendous flights of doves to the roosting grounds at the same time of year. For good shooting, it pays to keep an eye peeled for these concentrations.

LOCATING HUNTING AREAS

Preseason location of hunting areas for doves is not nearly as important as it is in duck and goose hunting. For one thing, the mourning dove is such a small bird that many hunters scorn hunting it at all, even though its fine flavor and sporting qualities more than make up for its lack of size, and it is not subjected to as heavy hunting pressure. Secondly, doves are so widely distributed that they are more readily available to hunters than most other game. However, if you live in a heavily populated area, it is often difficult to find a place where you can discharge a gun, much less find game to hunt. If this is the case, it is sensible to locate areas in advance.

Although it is easy to describe in general the kinds of places that attract mourning doves, it is not so easy to predict exactly which of these places may be most fruitful during the hunting season. Very few of our game birds are so dim-witted that they will return to the same areas day after day to be shot at repeatedly.

Even when not hunted, doves seem to leave an area for no apparent reason, and start using another in the immediate vicinity. I can recall watching these birds in North Dakota and Minnesota, when hunting them was illegal. They would work an area for a period of three or four days, disappear for a day or so, and then return. I have since learned that they were simply moving from one feeding or roosting ground to another, perhaps in an instinctive effort to minimize the various kinds of predation to which they are subjected. Locating hunting areas for these birds is largely a day to day business. You cannot be sure of finding doves again where you found them a week earlier.

Part of locating good hunting areas depends on being able to identify doves and to know what kind of habitat they use. Gravel pits, sandy lakes, rivers, and slough shores are excellent places to look as they offer the advantage of being open enough so that the birds may be easily seen and identified. Gravel pits are the most productive, with the rocky or gravelly lake shore running second. Sloughs are generally not as good as gravel pits because they have muddy shores and bottoms. I have seen mourning doves sitting out on the mud flats with kildeers and other shore birds. But this is far from their favorite habitat, and is usually good only if it is the closest water to an excellent feeding area. Rivers and streams can be productive, particularly if they are close to feeding or roosting areas.

Wooded or brushy areas, preferably close to water and feeding fields, are good potential areas. Usually these areas will provide the best shooting. Small groves lying low in valleys, or near slough bottoms, are excellent, particularly in the prairie states where tree cover is scarce. In heavily forested parts of the United States, I prefer the heaviest brushy thickets and brier patches near small woodland potholes or along streams. Shelter belts and groves between fields are also good and should not be overlooked in country where trees are scarce. Doves find abandoned farms attractive and in much of the West where many farm buildings have been abandoned, these present prime hunting spots.

Feeding fields are difficult to locate because the birds are so difficult to see. The best way to find doves in the field is to walk through it. You may not see the birds until they flush. Picked corn, the stubble of almost any small grain, and the legumes such as soybeans, navy beans, and peas, provide excellent food for doves and should also be considered. When looking for shooting locations of any kind, see how many aspects of good habitat you can find in one area. A tract containing water-filled gravel pits, grain stubble, heavy thickets, woods, and a deserted set of farm buildings, should be a natural hot spot.

Passes can be located after you have found roosting, watering, and feeding areas. This is done mainly by watching the area, and studying the movements of doves, particularly in the morning and evening. Like ducks, doves have certain patterns of flight which they tend to repeat, such as flying down a draw or valley, or across low-lying fields. Passes for doves are less sure than for ducks, however, because doves continually change their feeding and roosting spots.

HUNTING METHODS

Once you have learned the habits of mourning doves, hunting them reduces itself mainly to skillful shooting, and these birds are indeed among the most elusive of all targets. Their speed, the erratic path of their flight, and their small size, combine to make them extremely difficult to hit. When hunting doves, it is wise to bring three to four times as many shells as you would when hunting ducks or pheasants; proportionate to the bag limits, this might mean six or eight times as many shells would be needed. I have seen many good shooters go through two boxes of shells without touching a bird.

I have always preferred hunting doves from a blind, much in the manner of duck hunting. Although doves are not as shy as waterfowl, the best blinds for hunting them are of natural cover. I prefer the roosting areas for blind shooting. Usually there is enough natural cover so you have to do little more

A hunter raises his gun and takes aim at a mourning dove from the cover of high foliage. *Missouri Conservation Commission.*

than keep down as the birds come in. This shooting is usually done just before sunset; hence it is easier to get a good hide as the birds do not see well in the dim light.

Sometimes it is helpful to make a blind out of loose cover in front of the roosting thickets, giving you room to swing your shotgun, and a better chance at the birds before they fly into heavy cover. This type of blind can be made of whatever material is handy. Camouflaged suits or parkas are an aid, but are not essential to successful hunting. In the first day of the season, doves will come in unhesitatingly, even if one is exposed, but they quickly grow cautious.

Watering areas may also be hunted with the aid of blinds. When water is bordered by woods, the same principles of hiding apply as in roost shooting. The gravel pit, however, which is the best, demands a different solution. If these pits are completely devoid of foliage, the hunter must dig a shallow hole in which to hide. The effectiveness of the hiding place can be increased if a simple stake blind is used. Old burlap makes an effective blind when stretched over the hole. Sand blends with it well and can be used to weigh it down to hold it in place. The blind at a gravel pit can be placed either at the top of the pit, or at the bottom near the water, depending on how the birds are flying. In general, the blind is less conspicuous when placed at the bottom, and the birds are not likely to see you until they are well on their way to the water hole, and within gun range.

Blinds can also be constructed in the feed fields, but are less suited to field shooting than to roost or water shooting and are not particularly recommended. There is usually so much territory in which doves can feed in fields that it is hard to attract them to your particular spot. In the fields, it is best to use decoys.

I have found that these birds can be easily imitated with a decoy constructed of gray cloth, a piece of wire, and any kind of stuffing that you can find. I like to make the stand out of fairly soft but heavy wire that will take a good deal of bending. I make it long enough so that it can be wrapped around tree branches for use in roosting locations. The wire stands of these decoys can be pushed into the ground, and it is little extra work to put out a dozen or so of these where you are hunting. A camouflage suit or net offers plenty of cover for dove hunting in a stubble field, and the hunter can lie flat on his back, while he waits for birds to approach. It does not pay to dig pits, or construct other types of permanent blinds for doves, because of the irregular behavior of these birds.

The blind can also be used for pass hunting and this can be made of material at hand. Pass shooting is more difficult than shooting doves at their roost, water holes, or feeding fields, as they are usually flying much faster and higher. Doves can be hunted at any time of day from a good pass, though the heaviest flights occur early in the morning and at sunset. Whatever your method a second shot is useless, as the birds begin to dart and dive the minute they are shot at, offering an almost impossible target to hit.

"Walking them up" is another method of hunting doves. It provides many shots but as a rule the shots are even more difficult than in pass shooting, and

The intelligent black Labrador retriever, shown here with a dove, is also useful to the hunter as a flusher for upland game hunting. *Missouri Conservation Commission.*

Dove decoy, which is carved out of wood or made with stuffing and cloth cover, has a metal pin that can be imbedded in ground, and a screw-eye for hanging from tree.

they become progressively tougher as the birds get more wary and flush wildly. Grain stubbles, shorelines, and gravel roadsides are excellent places to walk up doves, especially in the morning and afternoon at the beginning of the season. As the season progresses, the more the birds are shot at, the farther out they flush, until most of them are rising at sixty-five to seventy yards out. Shots at such ranges can result in many lost cripples. The use of a good retriever is indicated here. I can see little use for a flushing dog or a pointer for this game and I have not heard of one being used for it.

Roosting areas, which may consist of groves, thickets, or clumps of trees, can be effectively walked at times, and birds can be seen in good numbers, especially during the middle of the day when they are taking their siesta. The main disadvantage to this kind of shooting is that birds flush with the result that there is heavy foliage between them and the gunner. It is helpful, when hunting in groves and thickets, to have one hunter walk on each side so that birds flying out of either side will offer a shot.

Dove hunting is obviously not a sport for the "meat hunter" and is not recommended to the novice shotgunner. It is, however, an excellent form of hunting for the expert or experienced shotgunner who is interested primarily in testing his shotgun skill, and who would like to get in some much-needed practice on live game before the seasons on waterfowl, and other larger game birds arrive.

6

Ringneck Pheasants

THE CHINESE ringneck pheasant (*Phasianus colchicus torquatus*) is actually only one of 150 different kinds of pheasants found throughout the world. These 150 pheasants can be classified into sixteen main genera. One of these genera is the junglefowl, an ancestor of our domestic poultry; another is the peacock. The genus which concerns us, however, is the true, or game, pheasant. The true pheasant can also be divided into two main species: colchicus and versicolor (green pheasant); the Chinese ringneck is a part of the species colchicus.

The colchicus species has five subspecies of importance to the hunter: the tarim, white-winged, black-necked, kirghiz (Mongolium), and gray-rumped (ring-necked). The gray-rumped or ringneck strain is predominant in the United States. The slight variation in different pheasants' color pattern, however, suggests that the black-necked, kirghiz (Mongolium) and even the green pheasant (the species is the versicolor) are a part of the ancestry in some states.

From the foregoing, you can see that the roots of the pheasant's family tree go quite deep. Archaeological findings have traced the pheasant back some 25 million years into the era of the giant mammoth and saber-toothed tiger. Records indicate that the Chinese people may have known of the pheasant three or four thousand years ago. Literature dated around 500 B.C. tells about long-tailed, ground-loving birds of brilliant plumage who were abundant along rivers flowing from the Caucasus mountains. The principle river was the Phasis (now called the Rion), so the Romans and Greeks called them the Phasianus avis, birds of the Phasis.

In their natural state, all pheasants except one (a species of the deep forests of the Belgian Congo), are found in Asia, Malaysia, neighboring islands, and in Europe in the Caucasus Mountains. The true, or game, pheasant is found from the eastern shores of the Black Sea, eastward to China and Japan.

The species colchicus, for the most part, was limited in its natural habitat to the mainland of Asia. In western Asia, the bird is a general red color with a reddish-brown lower back. The black-necked and kirghiz subspecies are generally found in western Asia. As one moves eastward across Asia, the gray-rumped birds are predominant. These birds vary in color. The mantle and sides of the body are always lighter and yellower than the breast; the lower back and rump are gray; the wing coverts are lavender-gray; the tail is greenish-buff with wider black bars. The Chinese ringneck is a member of this eastern group.

The versicolor species (green pheasants) are found in Japan. The mantle and under parts are entirely green. Most of the pheasants in the United States also have some of this coloring.

Sometimes albinistic pheasants, white with pink eyes, appear. These are mutations of the regular colors and are not to be confused with the fancy pheasants that are sometimes raised: the golden, Lady Amherst, Reeves and others.

The Chinese ring-necked pheasant came to the United States from Asia. The Greeks probably brought the first true pheasants into Europe about the seventh or eighth century B.C. These first pheasants were black-marked and were later taken from Europe to England (probably by Julius Caesar in the middle of the first century B.C.). These black-necked pheasants reached the United States in 1773 when a dozen pair were released on Nutten Island (Governor's Island), New York. Unfortunately, however, this and other early efforts to introduce them failed.

Finally, however, Judge Denny of Oregon imported some Chinese ring-necks into the Willamette Valley of that state in 1881. This was a historic occasion. Eleven years later, 50,000 birds were killed on the first day of the hunting season.

The success in Oregon whetted the desires of sportsmen across the United States. Many birds were subsequently brought over from the Old World. Most of these birds were a combination of the blackneck, kirghiz, and ringneck. From that time until this, the pheasant became very well established across the United States. As can be seen on the map, it is now found in forty-one states including Alaska and Hawaii. It is hunted in thirty-nine of these states, though it is very scarce in many places, where it is often hunted only on private preserves. States where the bird is very plentiful are also marked.

It must be emphasized, however, that pheasant densities vary from area to area and from year to year in any state. In North Dakota, for example, more birds were harvested by hunters in the western part of the state in 1959 than in the eastern part. In 1960, however, the number of birds bagged in the eastern part exceeded the total bagged in the western part.

IDENTIFICATION

The typical male pheasant in the United States weighs from 2½ to 3 pounds, the female about 2 pounds. Males may reach 34 inches or more with the tail exceeding 20 inches of this length. Hens are usually about 24 inches long, half of which is tail.

The plumage of the male is gaudy and brilliant. The head and upper neck are àn iridescent greenish-blue; there is a reddish "bloom" of bare skin around the eyes. The white ring around the neck and the long, pointed, tannish tail barred with black are distinguishing features. The sides are golden-buff spotted with black; the rump patch is a pale bluish color. The rusty back is spotted with black and cream markings; the breast is a rusty-bronze; the belly is greenish black. The coloration of the female is more drab with a mottled blend of browns with buff and dusky markings. The bird is darker above, lighter below.

The brightly colored male ringneck pheasant's most distinguishing features are the white ring around its neck and the long black-barred tail. *North Dakota Game and Fish Dept.*

RANGE AND DISTRIBUTION

Pheasants are found in areas where the soil is fertile and moist enough to support cover and food crops. Soil of low fertility will neither yield much corn nor harbor large numbers of pheasants. The bulk of pheasants are found on dark-colored soils.

Glaciated soils of high calcium content, such as are found in the northern plains, attract high pheasant populations. There are also high populations in some western unglaciated valleys.

Generally pheasants prefer the more northern states. Pheasants are a rarity in the eastern part of the United States south of the thirty-ninth parallel which runs just below the southern border of Pennsylvania. West of Arkansas and Louisiana every state has pheasants, but no large concentrations exist below the 37th parallel, which runs below San Francisco and along the southern border of Nevada, Colorado and Nebraska.

High pheasant populations are now generally associated with areas of grain farming that also have some rough pasture, timberland, and wasteland. The distribution of food and shelter is very important. If all the land is cultivated and planted, there is little cover for the birds to nest and roost, or to protect them from the elements in winter. If too much land is left in rough pasture,

Distribution of the ringneck pheasant

VERY PLENTIFUL
PLENTIFUL
PLENTIFUL ON LIMITED RANGE
SCARCE
NONE

O NO HUNTING
● HUNTING IN SEASON

timber or wasteland, food is scarce. Studies in Indiana show that the best pheasant range shows the following land-use pattern: at least 20 per cent in corn, at least 20 per cent in small grains, from 10 to 20 per cent in rotation pasture and hay, and not more than 9 per cent in rough pasture, timber, and wasteland.

Furthermore, pheasants like cover adjacent to feeding areas so the more edges of cover which surround grain fields the better. Thus, ten acres of shelter in a strip surrounding a forty-acre field is more effective than a ten-acre square in one corner.

Type of cover is very important, especially during the winter months. Brushy, ungrazed, unburned swale and potholes provide excellent winter cover, though these low spots flood out in the spring, sometimes destroying pheasant nests. Similarly, low deep drainage ditches filled with rushes and cattails offer excellent cover for pheasant during the winter months when the water in them is frozen solid. Uncultivated soil bank has provided millions of acres of good pheasant cover. Shelter belts, brushy woodlots, uncut fence rows, road borders and hay patches offer crowing, nesting, and roosting areas.

Habitat must be mostly free of factors and conditions which inhibit pheasant production and growth. For example, there must be enough un-disturbed nesting cover. Good cover that is overrun with livestock is useless for pheasant production. Similarly, mowing, plowing, or burning inhibits production. Night mowing of alfalfa is especially deadly; roosting cocks, hens, and chicks can be virtually wiped out in one night. Fall plowing destroys all

A winter concentration of ringnecks in South Dakota grain country. Ringnecks are found in abundance in brushy areas along the edge of broad grain and pasture fields. *South Dakota Dept. of Game, Fish and Parks.*

winter cover and food for pheasants, as does fall burning. Spring burning may mean death to nesting hens.

Adequate protection must also be available during the worst winter weather. Low temperatures alone are not serious to pheasants. But low temperatures combined with scarcity of food and cover and a rugged blizzard may be lethal. When available food is covered by heavy snow pheasants may starve, though they can go for periods longer than a month without food with no ill effects. Severe sleet storms smother birds not protected adequately. The sleet covers the mouth and nostrils, freezing them shut and smothering the birds. A driving snow which is blown under the feathers of birds, icing them up, may cause some birds to die of exposure and cold. None of these weather factors is serious, however, if adequate cover and food are available. This means that the best way to protect the birds is by habitat improvement.

NESTING AND REPRODUCTION

The first signs of the mating season are seen in February, March or early April, depending upon the locale. Flocks begin to break up and the birds leave their winter roosting sites to go to their nesting range. Cocks set up crowing territories which they defend against encroachment by other males. Often two cocks fight for a single territory, using their leg spurs. Only occasionally is the weaker cock killed; more often he retreats to find a territory of his own.

Each cock calls as many hens as possible into his territory, putting on an elaborate courting display by strutting, puffing out his feathers, and stretching one wing. Such courting is designed to entice a hen to stay within a harem, since females sometimes fly from one territory to another. In the best pheasant ranges, cocks usually average about three hens to a harem. Cocks are more than capable of fertilizing eight to ten hens, however. In captivity the cock can fertilize as many as fifty hens.

As the peak of the nesting season approaches, the number of crowing cocks increases, and the period between their calls becomes shorter. At the height of the crowing the period between calls is slightly under three minutes. The majority of calls are heard between forty minutes before and one hour after sunrise. Calling increases again toward evening, though it does not reach the extent of the morning period.

At the start of the nesting season, hens may drop a few eggs at random; usually these eggs are infertile. The reason for this random dropping is probably that egg development is faster than the physiological changes which cause nesting and incubation. Sometimes, too, a hen will construct an early nest, lay a few eggs, and then desert it. Sometimes one nest is used by two or more hens and so contains more than the normal clutch of twelve eggs. Broods usually range from eight to seventeen, but occasionally broods of over twenty are reported.

Nests are found in a variety of places. Hens apparently like alfalfa and clover fields, so many nests are destroyed each year by mowing operations. If a nest is destroyed during the egg-laying period, or early in incubation, the hen will renest. Each attempt, however, produces fewer eggs. However, each hen will raise only one brood during a summer.

Clutch of pheasant eggs. The hen deserts a nest when it is destroyed by predators and renests, producing a smaller brood. *North Dakota State Game and Fish Dept.*

The hen usually lays her twelve, olive-brown, unspotted eggs in about fifteen days. Incubation takes twenty-three to twenty-four days. The chicks leave the nest with the hen soon after hatching, for they are able to walk immediately. In a few days, the chicks begin to lose their downy covering and grow feathers. They fly fairly well by two weeks. Young males begin to color up by seven to eight weeks of age. A hen usually stays with her brood until the chicks are at least twelve weeks old. During early summer, roosters commonly stay in the vicinity of their harem's nests, though they do not help raise the brood, even if the hen is lost.

Like all upland birds, pheasant eggs need adequate moisture to hatch or they rot. In areas of limited rainfall, such as the Dakotas, total production of pheasants is closely related to total rainfall during the months of May and June. In a recent study in North Dakota, it was found that years that had above average rainfall in May and June also had better than average pheasant production of young. Furthermore, ample rainfall provides the cover and habitat so important to the survival of the pheasant. There can be too much rainfall, however. Indiana studies show that the fall population is lower when the average precipitation during April, May, June, and July approaches four inches. Excessive rain floods nests and chills chicks.

Studies in Michigan have revealed that low temperatures during incubation are detrimental to egg survival. The later in the incubation period the cold comes, the more sensitive are the eggs to exposure to the cold. Thus, during the second day of incubation, eggs will stand forty-eight hours exposure to 45° temperatures, but on the twenty-second day, only eight hours exposure. Furthermore, the colder the temperatures, the shorter the time the eggs can stand it. Production may thus be inhibited during an excessively cold

A covey of pheasants taking flight from a winter refuge. Pheasants often seek food in such woodlots during the winter months. *South Dakota Department of Game, Fish and Parks.*

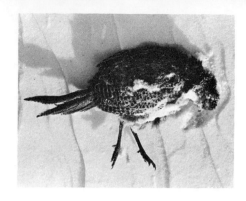

Result of a blizzard. Lack of adequate cover is the chief reason for pheasant mortality in winter. *North Dakota State Game and Fish Dept.*

spring. Furthermore, newly hatched chicks are more vulnerable to cold temperatures than are the eggs.

FEEDING PATTERNS AND HABITS

Young chicks generally start out on a strictly insect diet, living almost exclusively on grasshoppers, crickets, and other insects and larvae. When waste grain becomes abundant during the summer harvest, young pheasants shift to a grain diet. From late summer until the snows of early winter, waste grain is the most important item in the diet. Adults feed on corn, wheat, milo, oats, flax, soybeans and other cultivated grains, plus natural foods like insects and the seeds of ragweed, buttercup, smartweed, foxtail, and sunflowers. During periods of heavy snow, the diet is made up of tall-growing weeds with persistent seeds, or standing corn. If other food is not available, the birds are forced into heavier cover where they find less palatable foods such as sumac, poison ivy, bittersweet, viburnums, dogwood, and wild rose.

Pheasants need grit to grind the seeds they eat. If grit is not available, the gizzard retains harder seeds as substitute. Because grit is hard to obtain in winter, pheasants congregate along the edges of snow-plowed roads. A quick drive through good pheasant country will enable one to see them by the hundreds along the roads. Many are killed by cars.

LOCATING HUNTING AREAS

The movements of pheasants depend upon the season of the year, the time of day, cover, and food supplies. During the summer a cock and his harem remain with their chicks in a small area—usually less than eighty acres—especially if cover and food are ample. In the fall broods intermingle and move around a little more. In the winter pheasants flock up and may move to new locations to escape the cold blasts on the coverless open prairies. In the Dakotas birds move as much as ten miles, seeking river and slough bottoms, and cattails and sedges along lake shores. Furthermore, once settled, they may travel considerable distances from roosting cover to find food. Thus, even though they are homebodies, pheasants are quick to move from a poor habitat.

Pheasants, when flushed, flutter their wings violently and make loud cackling noises. *North Dakota State Game and Fish Dept.*

Pheasants normally roost on the ground in heavy cover. Sometimes, though not often, they roost in trees. Pheasants are up before daybreak and gather along edges of roads and fields looking for food and grit. As they can be found in the open at dawn, many hunters prefer to drive around and spot them, before getting out to hunt. In the early part of the morning, the birds feed and move around considerably. During the middle of the day they seek heavier, denser cover to rest. Occasionally, they move to dusting areas for short periods, or lie out in the sun in cold weather in stubble or hay fields. In the late afternoon, they begin moving about again, seeking food, grit, and returning to their roosting spots.

The mortality of pheasants is discouraging. If eleven out of twelve eggs hatch, an average of six chicks are left by the fall. Disease, predators and accident all take their toll. It has been shown time and again, however, that hunting cocks has very little to do with pheasant populations. This can be shown easily by the following.

Suppose one cock plus three hens produces nine cocks and nine hens (an average survival rate of six birds per hen by fall). If 50 per cent of the cocks are shot, the sex ratio remaining is 1:2. If 80 percent of the cocks are harvested, the sex ratio is 1:5. If 90 per cent of the cocks are harvested, the sex ratio after the season is over is 1:10, which is an adequate breeding combination for good fertility. Thus, closing a pheasant season doesn't help the populations much. Furthermore, few cocks live to the second season; closing the season and not shooting them means they just die from other causes. Three-fourths of any brood die within a year. Normally, pheasants cannot escape death for more than three or four years.

HUNTING METHODS

The first consideration is to find the birds. The preferred way is to locate your hunting areas before the season opens, asking permission of the landowner, or making arrangements with the manager of the preserve. If you are locating free hunting areas, drive through the countryside in the early morning or late evening, spotting pheasants within sight of the road. When concentrations of pheasants are spotted, survey the adjacent lands. Where are the best feeding areas such as cornfields or grain fields? Where is the best resting and roosting cover? It is wise to hunt the feeding areas early and late in the day and the resting areas during midday.

Very early and late in the day, many hunters prefer to road hunt. They drive around on small gravel roads spotting pheasants, then get out to shoot. This is the lazy man's way of hunting, but it does produce a lot of pheasants, especially early in the season. In between these hours the hunter will have to scout the cover.

If you go out alone, hunt the roads and the small cover patches, fence rows, very narrow strips of shelter belts, small grain strips or small areas of dry slough bottoms. To hunt large fields alone is futile. The pheasants run ahead, around, and away without flushing. The lone hunter with a dog may be in a slightly better position but even then it is difficult.

A good way to hunt fields is to form a party of hunters, the number depending upon the size of the fields to be hunted. Line up twenty to forty feet apart (the distance depending upon the thickness of the cover and whether or not there are dogs). To drive the field, place one or two hunters on the opposite edge of the field to "cap it off," that is, to prevent pheasants from running out that end and escaping. The party ought to move along erratically at a medium pace. Hunters often disagree on whether it is better to walk fast or slow. Some almost run across a field; others say that pheasants flush better if you walk deliberately, stopping often to give the birds a chance to become frightened and flush.

Personally, I hate to rush; many times pheasants flush when the hunters have all stopped for a talk. If you are using dogs, give them plenty of chance to sniff out and flush the birds. If you don't have dogs, and you have capped the field, your partners will get any birds escaping. Therefore, I prefer walking slowly, erratically, and in a zigzag pattern.

In driving, hunt one strip at a time, moving back and forth until the whole area is covered. If you can take only one turn, it is better to hunt into the wind, making it easier for the dogs to smell the birds.

When there is snow on the ground, the pheasants are easier to spot and to flush, since they feel less secure in the sparser cover. They can also be tracked and trailed when there is good snow cover.

Pheasant Hunting Dogs

I prefer labrador retrievers for hunting pheasants. I keep my dogs working back and forth in front of me within twenty-five yards distance with good success. It takes a smart pheasant to escape a flushing dog that has smelled the bird. Then too, a well-trained retriever can save many crippled birds, or birds downed in heavy cover. Fast-moving pointers can occasionally pin pheasants down, but many good pointers have a lot of trouble with them. While the dog is on point, the pheasant runs out and away from under his nose.

Whatever way you hunt, the modern cock pheasant is worthy game. He has learned to survive by wits and evasive tactics rather than by flying. He will sulk and hide, letting the hunter pass by within a few feet. He can run

A party of hunters drive a field. When hunting in this manner, it is best to place one or two hunters at the opposite end of the field to prevent the pheasants from getting away. *North Dakota State Game and Fish Dept.*

faster than a man, and will often cut around a line of hunters, or double back through the lines. He flushes with such a flutter of wings and cackling noise that he scares the most steel-nerved hunter. If wounded, he can disappear as if by magic in stubble only 4 inches high; squatting down, head low, he runs between the stubble at great speed.

Statistics show that the pheasant is a smart bird. Studies in Iowa during recent years revealed the following. The average hunter made about four trips per season. He killed an average of five birds during the season. It took him an average of two and a half hours of hunting for each bird killed. Over 18 per cent of the hunters were not able to kill a single pheasant.

7

Grouse of Prairies and Deserts

THE GROUSE FAMILY

There are eight grouse in the United States which are important to the hunter.

Ruffed (*Bonasa umbellus*)
Blue (*Dendragapus obscurus*)
Franklin's (*Canachites franklini*)
Spruce (*Canachites canadensis*)
Ptarmigan (*Lagopus lagopus*)
Sharp-tailed (*Pedioecetes phasianellus*)
Pinnated (*Tympanuchus cupido*)
Sage (*Centrocercus urophasianus*)

The heath hen (*Tympanuchus cupido cupido*), which is the eastern equivalent of the prairie chicken, is extinct and so is not listed.

Of the eight grouse listed above, the first five, ruffed, blue, Franklin's, spruce, and ptarmigan, can be classified as grouse of forests or mountains. The last three, sharp-tailed, pinnated, and sage, can be grouped together as grouse of prairies and deserts. The prairie and desert grouse will be discussed in this chapter; forest and mountain grouse will be discussed in Chapter 8.

SHARP-TAILED GROUSE—IDENTIFICATION

Other common names for the sharp-tailed grouse are sharptail, sharp-tailed prairie chicken, brush chicken, black foot, pintailed grouse, pintail, spiketail, spike-tailed grouse, sprigtailed grouse, white-bellied grouse, whitebelly, white grouse, willow grouse, prairie, and Columbian sharptail.

The sharp-tailed grouse, which has at least seven subspecies (one of which is the Columbian sharptail), is a large bird. Males are about 20 inches long and weigh up to 2 pounds. Females are slightly smaller.

The male and female are almost identical in appearance. This grouse is a short, plump bird, with a short, sharp tail. The two central tail feathers are longer than the rest, and are neutral colored on the male and cross-barred with black on the female.

As with all big grouse, the sharptail lacks any noticeable crest. The general color is gray and brown; the upper parts are grayish-brown with black and buffy markings; the under parts are buffy or whitish; the belly and under tail coverts are nearly white; feathers on the wings are each marked with a round spot of white. Breast feathers are marked with an irregular pattern of V-shaped markings of very dark brown. The legs are feathered to the toes; the toes themselves have a fringe of horny growth which serve as snowshoes. The head and neck are a rich buff with a whitish patch on each side of the neck and a whitish streak behind the eye. The cocks have purplish-colored air sacs on each side of the neck which are hidden by plumage when not inflated. The nape of the neck is marked with narrow transverse bars of blackish-brown. The throat is plain light buff. The upper mandible is a dark horn-color and the lower bill is flesh-colored. The iris is pale brown.

RANGE AND DISTRIBUTION

As can be seen on the map, sharptails are found in sixteen states, including Alaska. Eleven of these states have open season. The birds are very plentiful in Nebraska and abound on the eastern and western plains of Colorado, and on the open prairie lands of Montana and the Dakotas.

Distribution of the sharp-tailed grouse

NESTING AND REPRODUCTION

One of the most interesting aspects of the sharptail is its courtship behavior. In late winter or early spring, depending upon the weather, male sharptails gather in small groups of from two to thirty-five birds on the dancing grounds and commence their courtship displays, dancing and booming to attract the females. The dancing grounds are usually situated on ridges or knolls in a heavily-grazed pasture, or in a mowed hay field or other dry areas where the cover is short. Grounds may sometimes be found in tall, dense cover which the birds tramp down bare to make runways on which to perform. The same grounds are commonly used every year.

The male sharptails gather on the grounds early in the morning, from dawn to about two hours after sunrise. Usually they visit the grounds again late in the afternoon. After gathering, the birds first stand quietly about, then a cock half spreads his wings horizontally, lowers his head, fans out his tail, and, with air sacs distended to send forth his booming sounds, runs across the dancing ground. With the wings stiffly outstretched, the body in a horizontal position, the head pointing downward and the tail thrust straight up, the bird stamps his feet rapidly on the hard ground to produce a drumming sound. At the same time, his tail vibrates from side to side, the stiff feathers producing a rattling sound, and he utters a variety of hooting, clucking, cackling, and gobbling sounds.

Two sharp-tailed grouse begin their frenzied strut on the dancing grounds. This phenomenon constitutes the ritual of courtship among the birds. *North Dakota State Game and Fish Dept.*

The excitement of one cock is contagious and others follow his example. The birds circle right and left, charge back and forth, pass each other with bristled feathers. They bow, squat, and strut in a variety of postures with antics that resemble an Indian war dance. As their ardor increases, the birds jump wildly about, leaping over each other and occasionally fighting. Each cock tries to make as much noise and show as he can. When the females are attracted, the mating occurs both on and off the dancing grounds. The cocks never pair off like quail, and mate with all the hens they can.

Nesting activity usually starts the latter part of April and is carried on entirely by the females. Males take no part in building nests, incubating, or rearing the young. Nests are built upon the ground, usually in cover of grass, weeds, and low shrubs, and are simple hollowed out impressions in the ground, lined with grass and a few breast feathers. Over a period of two or three weeks the hen lays an average of twelve or thirteen grayish-olive eggs finely spotted with brown. The hen sits very closely, blending so well with its surroundings that it is almost invisible.

The eggs hatch in slightly over three weeks (about twenty-four days) and usually within a few hours of each other. In good weather, most broods hatch in early June; in cold and stormy weather, they may not hatch until late June or early July. After the chicks are dry, the mother leads them away from the nest. Usually, the chicks can run within a hour after hatching. If a first nest is destroyed, the hen will try to renest; but no more than one brood is raised each season. The young grow rapidly. They can fly before two weeks of age. They are completely feathered with juvenile plumage by six weeks. By sixteen weeks adult plumage has replaced the juvenile, except for two outer wing feathers which are retained until the second autumn.

From the time the young grouse leave their nest, their lives are in constant danger. Some may become separated from the hen and die of exposure; many are caught by hawks, crows, magpies, snakes, badgers, skunks, cats, dogs, and other predators. Some are killed by automobiles; farm machinery harvesting grain or mowing hay may kill others. Disease may kill some. So by the time the September hunting season arrives, only about five of a brood of eleven are left. And this is only in those cases where nesting and incubation are successful. Studies in Michigan show that out of 176 nests only 70 produce eggs hatched. In studies in South Dakota, the ratio of young per adult birds has varied from 5.6 young per adult during a year of the best production to 1:3 per adults in the year of poorest production.

Apparently, hunting has little effect upon sharptail populations from year to year. South Dakota game managers estimate that 25 per cent of the grouse are shot during an average hunting season, but spring censuses show that populations in heavily hunted areas do not change any more than those in areas hunted lightly or not at all. When hunters take some birds, fewer seem to die from natural causes. Average yearly losses of eggs and young chicks from all causes runs around 85 per cent.

In most of the best sharptail territory of the Dakotas, grouse production and populations are dependent partly upon annual rainfall. Above normal precipitation results in better plant growth and more cover, and consequently the grouse increase. South Dakota's best sharptail habitat lies within the zone which receives 15 to 19 inches of rainfall per year. Marked fluctuations in rainfall and cover conditions cause fluctuations in the populations. Temperature is also related to grouse production. The production of young grouse is better during a cool, moist growing season than during a hot, dry one. Grouse are adaptable birds, however. When the weather is hot, they seek the shade of woody cover or tall grass and weeds. When winter cold waves send the temperatures down to 30 degrees below zero, sharptails burrow beneath the surface of the snow where they may stay almost as long as a full day at a time.

FEEDING PATTERNS AND HABITS

These birds cannot survive where most of the land is cultivated. They are abundant in areas of sparse human population, where the land is covered with native vegetation. In fact, when more than 50 per cent of an area is cultivated, heavily grazed, or mowed, the area cannot support a high grouse population. This explains why grouse and pheasants are seldom found in the same areas. The best sharptail habitat consists of large expanses of grassland, more or less hilly, and broken occasionally by brushy draws and cultivated fields.

Grasses of tall or medium height, such as needlegrasses, bluestems, and wheatgrasses, are particularly important since these provide cover for nests and broods. Such weeds as goldenrod, goatsbeard, wild lettuce, wild licorice, sunflowers, and sweet clover furnish shelter, shade, and food for grouse when they concentrate along draws during hot summer weather. The upland growths of prairie clover, yucca, surf pea, and annual sages provide good cover.

Trees and shrubs are also important to sharptails for both cover and food. Skunkbrush, chokecherry, plum, wild rose, buffaloberry, cottonwood, American elm, green ash, snowberry, leadplant, and silver sage brush all provide cover and food, especially during the winter when sharptails move into brush or timbered areas. Sharptails like to feed on buds from willows and other trees, so their winter food supply is assured in adequate cover. During the spring and summer months, the grouse feed mainly on grass and weed seeds, green vegetation, insects, fruits of wild shrubs, and trees and waste grain.

The sharp-tailed grouse searching for food on the sparsely vegetated fields which are its habitat. The short, sharp tail rises dramatically white against the brown and grey body of the bird. *South Dakota Dept. of Game, Fish and Parks.*

LOCATING HUNTING AREAS

During the fall, sharptails begin to assemble in large flocks in areas where there are trees and brush for browsing, good grass, cover for roosting, and fields of grain stubble or corn for an easy food supply.

Banding studies reveal that sharptails will travel extensively to find adequate habitat and that females travel more than males. Males tend to stay nearer the dancing grounds all year. In Michigan, of thirty-two males released and recovered, the average distance traveled was four to nine miles (the long-est was fifty-four miles). Of twenty-seven females, the average distance traveled was about eight miles (the longest was twenty-four miles). Banding studies on the Missouri river bottoms in the Dakotas indicate that movements of grouse to and from the wintering grounds average about seven miles for males and thirteen miles for females. In early spring, the winter flocks disband and the birds scatter widely to breed.

HUNTING METHODS

The most difficult part of hunting sharptail is finding the birds, even in areas where they are abundant. On warm, sunny days, grouse can usually be found in clumps of brush and trees on north slopes, in draws, or on stream bottoms. Wooded creek or river bottoms are sometimes productive, but more often the small clumps of trees and shrubs in the heads of draws provide better hunting. Grouse especially like chokecherry and buffaloberry bushes. Brushy areas are not good late in the afternoon, however, because the grouse move out of them into the grassy flats or into stubble and corn fields to feed and roost.

On cool days, look for grouse on grassy flats and ridges. Areas with a mix-ture of light grazed grass and fairly dense grass plus weeds of moderate height are very productive.

Under the best of conditions, sharptail grouse are never overly abundant nor easy to hunt. The populations are lowest just before nesting time and may vary from four to nine birds per square mile, usually averaging six per square mile. When the hunting season opens in late September, there are usually sixteen birds per section of land in good grouse country.

Hunting success depends mainly on the population, amount of cover, ac-cessibility of areas, and weather. During dry summers when cover is scarce, populations decline, but grouse are more easily seen, so are easier to bag. Dur-ing periods of lush vegetation, production increases but the birds are harder to find. Studies in South Dakota over a period of ten years reveal that the number of grouse bagged per hunter has varied from three to about six birds. Studies of hunter success (with sharptails and prairie chickens combined) in the Upper peninsula of Michigan have revealed that the average number of birds flushed per gun hour was four; the average number shot per gun hour was less than one. This is not easy hunting in any man's language.

Dogs are useful on sharptails, especially in heavy cover. Early in the season, the birds will lie well to a pointing dog. Close-working flushing dogs are a real help also in finding and flushing the birds and in retrieving shot game.

Late in the season when the birds are more wary, or when they are in open country with sparse cover, or feeding in open stubble or grain fields, dogs—especially wide range dogs—are more hindrance than help. The birds are jittery and flush easily, and the real problem is getting within range.

Large parties of hunters without dogs can line up and tramp the cover with good success in fine grouse country. Lone hunters will do better to hunt the small brushy draws and cover patches. One hunter I know stops in the early morning on a high ridge or hill overlooking rolling grouse country and scans the area with binoculars, watching for the flying birds. He marks down promising areas and hunts them with good success.

Road hunting may bring some results, especially in the early morning or late afternoon when the birds are feeding in the open, and early in the season before the birds became too wild.

PINNATED GROUSE OR PRAIRIE CHICKEN

Other common names for this bird are squaretail, yellow legs, prairie hen, and prairie grouse. While the term prairie chicken is often used loosely to mean either the sharp-tailed grouse or the pinnated grouse, it is only properly applied to the latter.

There are four subspecies of true prairie chickens, as follows: Greater prairie chicken (*Tympanuchus cupido pinnatus*)—this is the most common and most widely distributed subspecies. Lesser prairie chicken (*Tympanchus cupido paleidicinctus*)—on a very limited range in western Oklahoma, the Texas panhandle, southwestern Kansas, eastern New Mexico and southeastern Colorado. Attwater's prairie chicken (*Tympanuchus cupido attwateri*)—of minor interest because of its very limited range along the Gulf of Mexico. Heath hen (*Tympanuchus cupido cupido*)—was the eastern prairie chicken, now extinct.

PRAIRIE CHICKEN–IDENTIFICATION

Most hunters have difficulty in distinguishing prairie chicken from sharp-tailed grouse, particularly when the birds are about the same size and when crossing and hybridizing has taken place. There are some differences, however.

The hunter can tell the difference between the sharptail and the prairie chicken by the latter's roundness of tail, as pictured at left. The prairie chicken is marked almost to the tail. *North Dakota State Game and Fish Dept.*

The sexes of the greater prairie chicken are alike in color, but they are both darker in color than sharptails. The upper parts are brownish-colored, marked with darker cross bars. The breast and belly are whitish, but much darker overall because they are marked with dark bars across the bird instead of the V-shaped markings which characterize the sharptail. Most of the V-shaped markings which are on the sharptail are only on the breast, but the dark bars of the prairie chicken go across and extend almost back to the tail. The tail of the prairie chicken is rounded, in contrast to the sharptail. A tuft of several feathers folded together projects from each side of the neck of the prairie chicken; these feathers are 3 to 4 inches long in the male and 1½ to 2 inches long in the female. The legs of prairie chicken are feathered to the feet, but the feathers are shorter and less dense than on the sharptail and the legs and feet of the chicken are a deep orange-yellow color. The large air sacs of the male prairie chicken are orange-colored rather than purplish as on the sharptail.

The lesser prairie chicken is like the greater except that it is smaller and somewhat paler in color. The lesser prairie chicken average 1½ pounds and 16 inches long, the greater prairie chicken 2 pounds and 18 inches long.

RANGE AND DISTRIBUTION

The prairie chicken was one of the most plentiful native birds of the United States. Greater prairie chicken were found in open country from southern Canada to Texas and from Colorado to eastern Ohio. Lesser prairie chicken covered the southwestern United States; Attwater's prairie chicken was in southern Texas and Louisiana and the heath hen inhabited the eastern states. But the plough, market hunting, and destruction of habitat took their toll. Market hunters often killed them at the rate of fifty to seventy-five per hunter per day. In 1874, market hunters shipped 300,000 grouse out of Nebraska alone. Thousands of birds were trapped. But the real cause of the decline was the growth of the population and increased cultivation of the land. Prairie chickens and machine farming just do not mix. Today, these fine birds are found in only thirteen states, with only six states allowing some shooting. In states where shooting is allowed, the birds can be found in only limited areas.

There is some difference in type of habitat preferred. Both sharptails and prairie chickens like large areas of uncultivated land covered with a good growth of native grasses and weeds. But brush and trees are not as necessary to the prairie chicken as to sharptails. Chickens love the wide open spaces. They are also more gregarious, forming large flocks of a hundred or more in the fall when migrating to the wintering grounds.

NESTING AND REPRODUCTION

The courting, nesting, and reproductive habits of the prairie chicken are similar to the sharptail. The males gather on the same type of booming grounds in early spring and go through the same ritual to attract the females.

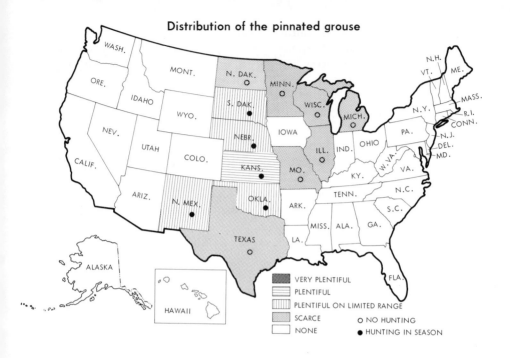

Distribution of the pinnated grouse

Nesting habits are about the same as those of sharptails, and the number of eggs and young produced are similar. The rate of growth and life cycle is identical.

FEEDING PATTERNS AND HABITS

Food habits of prairie chickens are similar to those of sharptails. During spring, summer, and early fall they eat large quantities of insects, especially the young birds. Green vegetation and wild fruits are eaten as long as available. Small grain provides food in late summer, fall, winter, and early spring but corn is the preferred winter food. Buds and twigs are occasionally eaten in the winter but they are not as important for prairie chickens as for sharptails.

HUNTING METHODS

In the first few days of the hunting season, chickens hold well to dogs, flushing within shooting distance. But as the season progresses, the birds become wilder, flushing at increasingly longer ranges. In the heaviest grass, good dogs certainly help in finding, flushing, or retrieving. But in more open spaces dogs do as much harm as good, since with dogs it is harder to get within range of the flocks. Under such circumstances, full choke guns with number 6 to 4 shot help in reaching the birds that flush wild.

A hunter scans the horizon for sharptails and prairie chickens. They prefer vast uncultivated plains, far from civilization. *North Dakota State Game and Fish Dept.*

SAGE GROUSE

Other common names for the sage grouse are sage hen, sage chicken, and cock of the plains.

SAGE GROUSE–IDENTIFICATION

This bird is the largest of the American game birds, except the turkey, weighing from 5 to 8 pounds and measuring 20 to 30 inches in length, with hens considerably smaller. The male and female are similar in coloring except the colors of the male are somewhat darker and more pronounced, particularly during the mating season. This bird is gray-brown, mottled with black, gray and white. The white breast and black belly characterize the big cocks. This bird is the only grouse having many long, sharply-pointed tail feathers. Like other grouse, the feet are feathered to the toes. The throat of the male is dark, bordered with white at the rear. Greenish-yellow air sacs are found on each side of the neck; the lower front is covered with short, stiff, scale-like white feathers; the sides of the neck are adorned with black and white plume-like feathers. The female lacks the air sacs, has a grayish-white chin and upper throat and a grayish-mottled neck and breast.

RANGE AND DISTRIBUTION

This bird is very much a grouse of the open, semi-arid sage brush country.

117

This sage grouse is easily identified as a cock by its black throat and white breast. As the bird feeds mainly on sagebrush, the flavor of the older birds is apt to be bitter. *North Dakota State Game and Fish Dept.*

It is found in thirteen states of the western United States. Eleven of these states allow hunting for this bird.

NESTING AND REPRODUCTION

Like other prairie grouse, the male sage grouse gather at established strutting areas in March, April, and early May to drum, croak, dance, and strut to attract as many females as possible. The male holds his drooping wings away from his sides, raises and spreads his tail which he opens and closes like a fan, all the while moving from side to side. At the same time, the air sacs are inflated and deflated like a bellows; when distended, the hair on them

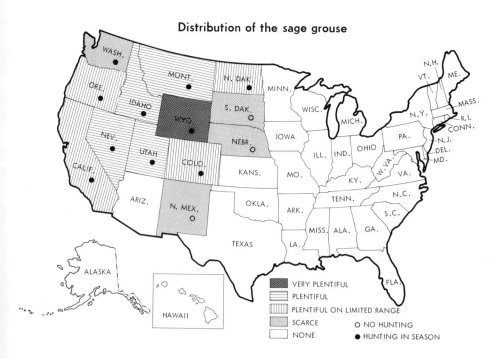

Distribution of the sage grouse

VERY PLENTIFUL
PLENTIFUL
PLENTIFUL ON LIMITED RANGE
SCARCE
NONE

O NO HUNTING
● HUNTING IN SEASON

The sage grouse, recognized by their formidable pin-pointed fantails, congregate on the dancing grounds. *North Dakota State Game and Fish Dept.,*

bristles out at right angles. The expelling of the air causes coarse grunting and croaking sounds; the cock meanwhile dances about pompously or throws himself forward on his balloon-like air sacs and pushes himself along.

After mating takes place, nesting is accomplished over a two to three week period; a shallow depression lined with grass or twigs is made under sagebrush. The female then lays five to ten olive-buff colored eggs spotted with brown. Incubation requires twenty-five days. The young chicks are able to run when fifteen minutes old, but the mother broods them throughout the summer while the males gather in groups. By late autumn the birds are fully grown.

FEEDING PATTERNS AND HABITS

The principal foods of the sage grouse are vegetable, since the birds have no thick-walled gizzards in which to grind foods. Their main diet is sagebrush leaves and shoots, supplemented with some insects, leaves and flowers of clover, dandelion, grasses, and other plants. Because of a preponderant amount of sagebrush in the diet, the older birds have a bitter, unpleasant taste, particularly if not cleaned and drawn right after killing.

HUNTING METHODS

Sage grouse are found fairly near water, in sagebrush, sometimes at high elevations. Especially in late summer the birds tend to concentrate around springs or the areas where green feed and water are available. In late fall, sage grouse form large packs and begin their short migrations to wintering areas; often to valleys, or to timber areas where they are sheltered.

These birds are very slow about flushing when found away from civilization. But after being disturbed frequently, they will flush farther away and fly for longer distances. In fact, they fly so far that there is little hope of marking down and following up singles. Once flushed, their take off is slow and labored, but the birds gather speed rapidly.

Many hunters shoot only the young, smaller and more tender birds. Old birds are often too tough to chew. The most successful hunters cover a large area as flocks are widely scattered. Always, however, select sage basins not more than a mile from water. A good pointing or flushing dog will help some in locating birds. Parties of hunters can line up abreast and walk through large areas of sagebrush. Another way to hunt is to ride a truck or jeep across sage brush country, trying to spot birds. After spotting them, the hunters then get off quickly to stalk and to shoot.

8

Grouse of Forests and Mountains

RUFFED GROUSE

Common names for the ruffed grouse are partridge, pheasant, birch partridge, drumming grouse, grouse, long-tailed grouse, mountain pheasant, shoulder-knot grouse, tippet, white-flesher, wood grouse, brush pheasant, native pheasant, willow grouse and willow pheasant. There are twelve subspecies of ruffed grouse in the United States and an additional one in Nova Scotia. Because there are only slight differences between them, however, I will group all of them together and refer to them all as ruffed grouse (*Bonasa umbellus*). The generic name *Bonasa*, meaning bison, may be suggested by the drumming sounds which sound like a herd of buffalo or by the sound of their wild, headlong flight. The species name, *umbellus*, means umbrella, referring to the neck ruff which can be raised and spread like an umbrella.

IDENTIFICATION

The ruffed grouse is a fairly large upland game bird and weighs about the same as a small chicken. An adult male is 16 to 19 inches long and weighs from 1 to 2 pounds. The head, back of the neck, and upper parts of the body are a light chestnut brown spotted with buff, gray, white and black. Feathers on the crown are barred with black and rise to a crest on both the cock and hen (less rise on hen). A line of light buff beginning at the bill extends beyond the eye to the rear of the bird's head. The throat is light buff, barred with brown. At the base of the neck on each side, tuffs of long broad, black feathers, sometimes tipped with brown, form the ruff or collar. This collar may have a metallic or iridescent sheen or be a reddish-brown without sheen. Just above the ruff, and extending across the chest below the throat, is a series of four or five dark, narrow, irregular rings, separated by light buff. The lower back and rump are marked with reddish-brown and with a series of oval buff spots encircled with black.

121

The black band across the tail of the male ruffed grouse makes it easily identifiable. He lies on the hunter's jacket, the result of a successful day's hunt. *North Dakota State Game and Fish Dept.*

The long tail is gray or brown. If gray, it is mottled with black and crossed by six or seven narrow bands of blackish-brown and one wide subterminal bar. If brown, the tail is crossed by irregular buff bands, bordered above and below by narrow bands of black. The subterminal black band across the tail is bordered on each side by gray mottled with black.

The breast is whitish, washed with pale brown or ochre, and marked with transverse bars of dark brown. The pale, whitish-ochre sides and abdomen are marked with large wedge-shaped spots of brown. The feathers under the tail and on the thighs are buff tinged with gray. The legs are feathered to the hind toes; the feet are brownish-black. Small, horny projections grow on the side of the toes each winter and serve as snowshoes which are shed in the spring.

The foregoing description applies generally to most ruffed grouse, though the different subspecies range in overall coloration from gray to brown to red.

RANGE AND DISTRIBUTION

Ruffed grouse are more widely distributed and hunted than any other grouse in the United States. Note from the map that they are found in thirty-four states. Twenty-nine of these states allow hunting.

NESTING AND REPRODUCTION

The courtship habits of the ruffed grouse are somewhat similar to other grouse. The cocks select drumming sites to which they return year after year. The chosen spot may be a long large rock, old stone fence, or stump, but it is always selected to give a fairly clear view of the surroundings.

Once the site is chosen, the cock mounts his perch, gives a few introductory wing flaps, and then—with body held erect begins an increasingly rapid beat

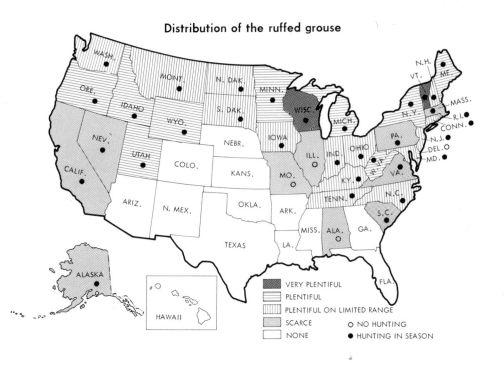

Distribution of the ruffed grouse

VERY PLENTIFUL
PLENTIFUL
PLENTIFUL ON LIMITED RANGE
SCARCE   ○ NO HUNTING
NONE   ● HUNTING IN SEASON

of the wings until they are just a blur. The drumming sound is produced by the rush of air through the opened primary feathers.

Suddenly the beating ceases; the cock stands erect, listening and waiting for a hen to appear. At first, the cock cannot be certain whether the appearance of another grouse is a cock or hen, so he stands ready either for a fight or for courtship. He advances with ruff extended, wings drooping, tail erect and fanned out, uttering a hissing sound as he shakes his head rapidly. If the arrival is a cock, a long fight may ensue, ending in the weaker bird being driven off. If a hen arrives, the cock struts with fan extended, pecking her gently on the bill. The hen is soon receptive to his attentions and mating occurs.

The cock is polygamous and attracts as many hens as possible, each of which disappears after mating to build a crude nest of twigs, dead leaves and grass, under a tree, brushpile, log, overhanging rock, or other protection. From eight to fifteen eggs, pale cream or brown (sometimes blotched or spotted with dusky markings), are laid and incubated for twenty-three to twenty-four days. After about a week, the hen begins to remove any infertile eggs from the nest. Often she will cover herself or her nest with leaves or grass to avoid detection, especially early in the incubation period.

Nesting occurs during late April, May, or June; the peak of the hatching is in June and July. The females raise the brood without any assistance from the male, who maintains a solitary existence throughout the summer. As with other grouse, the chicks follow the mother in search of food shortly after the natal down is dry. If the hen is discovered nesting or brooding, she will use the broken wing trick, flopping around pitifully to try to lure the intruder away from the nest or chicks.

But in spite of nature's provisions, many chicks are lost. Snakes, skunks, raccoons, opossums, squirrels, chipmunks and other predators rob many nests. Many chicks fall into water-filled holes while following the mother, or they get wet and chilled during a heavy rain and die. Many birds are also killed by automobiles.

Fortunately, however, flight quills sprout soon on the baby grouse and they are able to fly within ten days. They then fly up into the trees to roost and are much safer. Gradually, the down is replaced by pin feathers, then by juvenile and adult feathers. The brood usually stays together until fall. The family groups then begin to break up and to mix with others forming large wintering flocks. Late in July, the adult birds moult and lose the power of flight. During this period, they seek shelter in the heaviest cover and move about very little in order to avoid detection by their enemies. By September new plumage has grown and the birds emerge from their hiding places. Sometimes the young cocks return to their drumming logs, not to attract mates, but to display their male vanity.

FEEDING PATTERNS AND HABITS

The diet of ruffed grouse is a very broad one but they prefer berries of all kinds when available. During the spring and summer they also eat tender shoots of plants, green leaves, and small insects. The young birds especially like insects.

In the autumn, the birds add nuts to their diet. They eat a great deal of grain and seeds. Also, during the winter, the birds feed a lot on seeds and buds of deciduous trees.

LOCATING HUNTING AREAS

The ruffed grouse is nonmigratory and seldom moves beyond a half-mile radius from one spot. So it usually selects areas of ample food supply. It particularly likes brushy woodland areas adjacent to streams and springs. Thickets of deciduous trees and shrubs interspersed with conifers provide the most desirable habitat. Bramble patches or dense low thickets bordering clearings are wonderful spots in good weather. It frequents sunny hillsides in the summer but drops back down to the lowlands to the shelter of mixed evergreens and deciduous cover in the winter. Old orchards and abandoned farms that provide tender shoots, plant life, and fruit are fine spots in the spring, summer, and early fall. Little-used roads or paths are good places for dusting. One favorite haunt is a cut over stand of hardwoods interspersed with evergreens. On rainy or stormy days, the ruffed grouse seeks the shelter of tall conifers and dense thickets.

This bird usually feeds from daybreak to just before noon, then seeks a sheltered spot to rest and dust. By midafternoon it resumes feeding and continues until time to roost at dusk.

HUNTING METHODS

In finding ruffed grouse to hunt, it helps to scout likely areas before the season begins. Driving out in the country in early spring to listen for the booming beat of drumming grouse is a good idea. Look for likely feeding areas not far from water, and for thick evergreens and thickets where grouse may seek protection in winter. Apple orchards or berry patches with fine ground cover are marvelous hunting spots. In inclement weather, you will have to hunt the thicker evergreens near the feeding, resting, and dusting sites.

This bird is both a challenge and a delight to the hunter. It will hold as well to dogs as any other upland game bird, so by all means try to use close-ranging pointers or even flushers. Ruffed grouse dislike flying, but when flushed often, become so jittery one can hardly get a shot. The bird always flushes toward heavy cover and often puts a tree or other object between itself and the hunter. Furthermore, it flies fast and low, generally in a straight line, not more than 200 or 300 yards and usually a shorter distance. Remember also that high flyers often light in conifers.

One answer to the problem of trying to shoot ruffed grouse in cover is to hunt just the small woodlots, those that are bordered by open areas such as pastures, roads, and clearings. Hunters should move in from one end and by the time they reach the other end, the birds will have to flush into the open, giving a clear shot.

Some hunters will not hunt ruffed grouse until the leaves are off the trees. However, heavy leaf cover forces the birds to rise above the trees, thus providing easier shots. The important thing is to plan where and how you go into cover so that when you flush the birds you will have a chance to shoot.

For hunters without dogs, drives can be organized. One gunner ought to be stationed at the end where the birds are most likely to flush, while the other hunters line up and walk through, driving the birds out of the cover. The party ought to move in a hesitant, erratic manner, as this unnerves the birds and causes them to flush easier.

Ruffed grouse, as other game birds, are always easier to find in the early mornings and late afternoons, since they are often hidden in dense cover during the midday hours.

Winged birds will run after falling down, so, if a bird spins, flutters or spirals down, look for the cripple in a wide radius around the spot in which the bird was marked down. Retrievers help tremendously in recovering crippled birds. As in quail hunting, never shoot more than 50 or 60 per cent of the birds from one covey so as to leave breeding stock for the next spring.

Under the best of hunting conditions, ruffed grouse are difficult to bag. Studies in Michigan reveal that the number of grouse flushed per gun hour is usually about two. The North Carolina Resources Commission reports that

Hunters examine their bag of ruffed grouse. As with ringneck pheasants, ruffed grouse can be hunted without dogs by driving a patch of woods which is "capped off" by one of the hunters. *North Dakota State Game and Fish Dept.*

the average hunter in that state makes about two trips per season, shoots four to five ruffed grouse per season, and has an average kill per trip of about two birds.

BLUE GROUSE

Other common names for the blue grouse are dusky grouse, sooty grouse, pine grouse, pine hen, mountain grouse, gray grouse, fool hen, and hooter. This is the second largest grouse, the largest being the sage grouse. A blue grouse male is about 21 to 22 inches long and weighs up to 4 pounds. Females are somewhat smaller.

IDENTIFICATION

Male birds are dark gray, or slatey-black above, with mottled brown on the wings; the under parts are pale bluish-gray or bluish-ash marked with white on the sides of the neck and flanks. The legs and feet are covered with gray feathers. The tail is brownish and has a narrow gray terminal band and a black tip. During the mating season an orange comb develops over the eye of the male and colored air sacs (orange to red in color) show on the sides of the neck. Females have less pronounced colors, a brown back instead of gray-blue, and lack the orange comb and air sacs.

126

RANGE AND DISTRIBUTION

As can be seen on the map, this bird is found in twelve states including Alaska; it is hunted in eleven states. While abundant in some areas, it is not hunted as much as some other species because of its inaccessibility along the higher forested uplands and mountain slopes. Heavy stands of fir, pine, spruce and other conifers must be present to offer good roosting and escape cover.

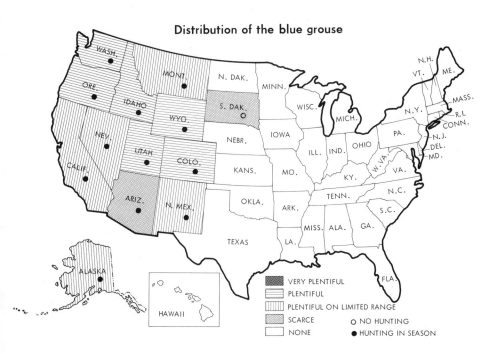

Distribution of the blue grouse

NESTING AND REPRODUCTION

Blue grouse are sometimes called "hooters" because of the low-pitched hooting sound the male makes during the mating season. Hooting usually takes place from the concealment of a thick conifer and is accompanied by the inflation of the brightly-colored air sacs. After hens are attracted, the male struts on a log or on the ground with wings drooping, tail held stiffly erect and air sacs distended. He suddenly bows, expelling the air from the sacs and producing a resonant booming sound. Males are polygamous, and they will battle over hens.

After courtship and mating, which takes place from April through June, a hen goes into seclusion, builds her nest and proceeds with egg laying. The nest is little more than a crude collection of grass and pine needles placed in a depression in the ground. It is usually located near the edge of timber, under

The blue grouse roosts in the inaccessible high forested mountains of the West. If he strays lower down, though, he presents a vulnerable target to the hunter. *Wyoming Game and Fish Dept.*

a log, or near the base of a tree or shrub. Six to ten cream-colored or buff-colored eggs, finely spotted with brown, are laid and are incubated over a period of twenty-four days. Most young hatch in late May or June, with the peak of the hatching coming about the middle of June. The small birds are cared for only by the female; the males move to higher timbered areas when nesting begins. The chicks grow rapidly, but young grouse are usually very timid, flying only to the nearest tree for escape.

During most of the summer the brood stays together, sometimes intermingling with other broods, but occupying the same areas along slopes, near meadows, deciduous cover, and water. One study in Montana reveals that most movements of juveniles, from July to September, are restricted to areas of one-half mile or less.

As the fall approaches, however, males and broodless females move first from summer ranges to higher elevations, followed by singles or small groups of juveniles from broods. The broods disperse and climb to higher elevations.

FEEDING PATTERNS AND HABITS

At first it seems strange that these grouse move to higher elevations with the arrival of winter. The reason is that they live off of evergreen needles during the winter, and must ascend the mountains to find the dense timbered areas which furnish conifer needles for food as well as protection. During periods of severe weather birds have been known to remain for days or weeks in the same dense Douglas fir tree.

As with all upland game birds, the mortality rate of blue grouse is very high. Population studies indicate a 67 per cent mortality of the young by August and a 31 per cent yearly death rate of adult males. Hunting usually has only a minor influence on populations; banding studies in two successive years in Montana revealed that only 7 per cent of the birds were shot by hunters one year and 12 per cent were shot another year.

LOCATING HUNTING AREAS

Hunting success depends somewhat upon the altitudinal migrations of the grouse by the time the season opens. Grouse are more vulnerable at lower elevations. In one year in Montana, 66 per cent of all birds shot were bagged at elevations above 7400 feet. That year it took about six hours to bag each bird. The following year, only 17 per cent of the grouse were killed at elevations above 7400 feet. That year it took only three and one-half hours to bag each bird. It would seem, therefore, that in years of early migrations to higher elevations, hunting blue grouse becomes more difficult. This can be partially compensated for by opening hunting seasons early enough in September.

The blue grouse's summer diet of insects, berries, tender plants, worms, and seeds makes it fine eating during the fall hunting months.

Blue grouse are sometimes called fool hens, because in the primitive state they have no fear of man and are easily approached. When the hunter approaches, they remain perched on limb of tree and are easily killed. If hunted regularly, however, they grow jittery and wild and therefore become a very sporting bird. They are fast, graceful flyers. When flushed, they pitch off a tree or ridge with a fast wing beat, then set their wings and glide down the mountain slope a short distance and alight in a conifer or thicket. They much prefer to fly downhill when flushed, unless they are already in a valley.

With the first warm days of spring, even while much snow remains in the mountains, the grouse flies back to the low country where green grass is sprouting. Throughout spring and summer, blues are widely scattered on foothill slopes and creek bottoms.

HUNTING METHODS

The methods for blue grouse hunting depend somewhat on the wildness of the birds. In remote areas, blues are often quiet enough to be picked off tree limbs with a .22 rifle. When flushed, the birds make for good wing shooting with shotguns. The downhill flight is fast; the birds often put the cover of trees between themselves and the hunter, so they are hard to shoot. Pointing dogs can be used to find the grouse in heavy thickets and cover, and the birds will lie well to a dog. When the birds are perched high up in tree limbs, however, dogs often miss the scent. Often a hunter will see the birds himself, or first be aware of them when they flush from a nearby tree. Retrievers are a big help in flushing from low cover and in retrieving downed birds.

The hardest part of hunting blues is climbing mountains to find them. It is possible to hike around the mountains for hours before finding concentrations of birds. However, like all grouse, these birds will usually not stray too far from streams or springs during the fall, so open ridges, brushy draws or timbered areas near water are likely spots. The later the time of year, the higher the hunter will usually have to climb to find birds. If you find any birds, there may be over 500 birds in the area. Before hunting blue grouse, I suggest you ask the state fish and game department where the areas of largest concentrations are found.

FRANKLIN'S GROUSE AND SPRUCE GROUSE

Some biologists classify Franklin's grouse as a subspecies of spruce grouse, calling Franklin's grouse *Canachites canadensis franklinii* and the spruce grouse *Canachites canadensis*. However, most authorities classify Franklin's grouse as a separate species, even though differences between it and the spruce grouse are slight. Other common names for Franklin's grouse are fool hen, Franklin's spruce grouse, mountain grouse, Tyee grouse, and wood grouse. Common names for the spruce grouse are spruce hen, fool hen, black grouse, Canada grouse, cedar partridge, spotted grouse, swamp grouse, swamp partridge, wood grouse, and wood partridge.

IDENTIFICATION

Both Franklin's and spruce grouse are small and dark, averaging 15 to 16 inches long and ¾ to 1½ pounds in weight. The adult male has a gray back, head, neck, and shoulders barred with black; the throat and chest are black and barred with white; the under parts are black barred with white. The flanks are streaked with white and brown; the sides of the rump are barred with white. The feet are completely feathered down to the toes. There is a small red comb over the eye of the male.

The female is blackish above, light brown and white below, with considerable barring and mottling of black, white and rusty-brown over the entire body. She lacks the reddish comb over the eye, also. The only real difference in appearance between the spruce grouse and Franklin's grouse is in the coloring of the tip of the tail, which is white on the Franklin's grouse, and orange-brown on the spruce grouse.

The male spruce grouse stands on a log in the big timber country he calls home. These birds are so unwary that they can be called the fool hens of the grouse. *Wisconsin Conservation Dept.*

RANGE AND DISTRIBUTION

Both of these birds inhabit the higher elevations of the big timber and high mountains. They are found in the northern states, with Franklin's grouse localized in northwestern states and spruce grouse also found in four states of the north-central and northeast United States. Both grouse are found in Canada and Alaska.

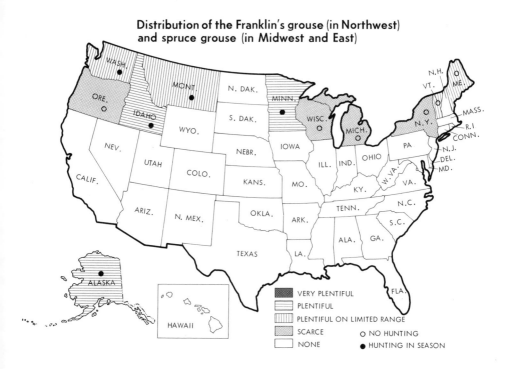

Distribution of the Franklin's grouse (in Northwest) and spruce grouse (in Midwest and East)

VERY PLENTIFUL
PLENTIFUL
PLENTIFUL ON LIMITED RANGE
SCARCE   O NO HUNTING
NONE   ● HUNTING IN SEASON

NESTING AND REPRODUCTION

Because of the high elevations at which this grouse nests, broods come a little later than for some other species. Nesting occurs in May and June; the nest consists of a shallow depression on the ground lined with grass or evergreen needles and located near a convenient thicket or mountain meadow stream. A clutch of eight to fifteen eggs, buff or pale brown in color, spotted with dark brown, is completed by mid-June. Incubation takes a little over three weeks, so the young appear in early July. The female incubates the eggs and cares for the brood while the male goes off by himself.

The males perform their courting dance and flight but ordinarily do not select a rock, stump, or log for drumming, preferring instead to find a small open area across which it can fly back and forth. At the end of each flight, the bird drops to the ground to strut about in full display with tail spread fanwise and wing tips dragging the ground, after which it flies up to a perch with a whirring of wings. Drumming usually takes place while the bird is in the air during the courting flight.

FEEDING PATTERNS AND HABITS

For food, these birds prefer the pungent needles of the pine, spruce, fir and balsam, during all seasons of the year. Insects, berries, seeds and tender leaves are available all summer, but few are eaten.

131

LOCATING HUNTING AREAS

It was once commonly believed that these grouse could be found only in the deepest and darkest black spruce and cedar swamps. Such is not the case, however. Observations in Minnesota reveal that the birds are most commonly found in jack pine, followed by black spruce, balsam, and tamarack, in that order.

In general, this preference for uplands and jack pine holds true all year, though the birds used black spruce during the summer about as much as jack pine. Furthermore, it has been shown that cedar, red pine, white pine, and white spruce are relatively unused as cover.

HUNTING METHODS

Unfortunately these are not very sporting birds; they are truly the fool hens of the grouse family, often refusing to flush or fly even to get off a road as a car approaches. Many are killed on logging roads during the winter simply because they will not move off the road to let pulp trucks pass. When perched in a tree these birds fall easy prey even to the beginning hunter. The Indians used to catch them by putting nooses on the ends of poles and slipping the loops over the heads of the birds. When the birds can be made to fly, however, they can be missed because of heavy cover. The main reason these birds have survived is that they live in out-of-the way timbered areas where man does not often penetrate. The birds are completely protected by law in many states.

PTARMIGAN

There are three major species of ptarmigan; the willow ptarmigan (*Lagopus lagopus*); the rock ptarmigan (*Lagopus mutus*); and the white-tailed ptarmigan (*Lagopus leucurus*).

Common names for the willow ptarmigan are common ptarmigan, snow grouse, snow partridge, white grouse, and willow grouse. This bird is difficult to describe since it moults three times each year and the plumage changes continually. In general, the summer plumage of the adult male is chestnut or cinnamon brown on the head, neck, and breast. The crown is spotted with black and the neck and chest are barred with black. The back and upper parts are reddish-brown, but broadly and thickly barred with black. This area and the wing coverts are always blotched and spotted with varying-sized areas of white. The under parts are nearly white. The summer plumage of the female is a mixture of tawny-brown and gray, heavily barred and spotted with dusky markings. The wings are mostly white with some brown. The under parts are white with barred markings. Legs and feet are completely feathered.

During the winter, however, the body of both sexes is snowy white. Only the tail feathers are black with white tips.

The willow ptarmigan breeds across the northern tundra from Greenland to the Aleutian Islands. In the winter migrations may occur as much as

500 miles from the breeding areas, though shorter movements are more common. Willow ptarmigan are very commonly found over most of Canada, particularly in the Yukon and Northwest Territories. In the United States, they are found only in Alaska, where they occur in abundance.

Rock ptarmigan are slightly smaller than the willow ptarmigan. In summer, the upper parts, except the wings and tail, are brownish-yellow barred with blackish-brown. The under parts of the male, except the sides and breast, are white. Under parts of the female, and the wings and tail of both sexes, are white. In the winter, all adults are pure white except for black tail feathers and a black line that extends from the bill to behind the eye.

The range of the rock ptarmigan often overlaps that of the willow ptarmigan. It is found only in Alaska in the United States, but abounds in Canada, particularly in the Yukon and Northwest Territories. The more southern provinces of British Columbia, Alberta, Quebec and Ontario have fewer of both rock and willow ptarmigan.

Common names for the white-tailed ptarmigan are mountain quail, Rocky Mountain snow grouse, snow grouse, and white quail. This is the only species of ptarmigan found south of Canada (see map). Six states, including Alaska, have this bird. It is found in the Rocky Mountains from Canada to New Mexico and is even prevalent in Colorado at high elevations. It is classified as a game bird in Alaska, Washington, and Colorado.

The white-tailed ptarmigan is the smallest member of the ptarmigan

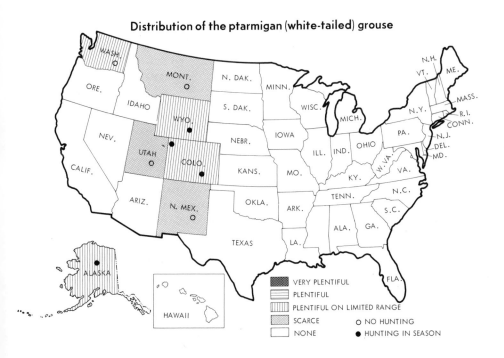

Distribution of the ptarmigan (white-tailed) grouse

VERY PLENTIFUL
PLENTIFUL
PLENTIFUL ON LIMITED RANGE
SCARCE   O NO HUNTING
NONE   ● HUNTING IN SEASON

family, being no more than 13 inches long. During the summer, adults have the head, neck, back, and breast finely marked with grayish-brown, white, and black. These markings vary greatly, however, as there are so many color variations. The tail, most of the wings, and the lower parts of the breast down are pure white. The legs and feet are entirely feathered. The bill is black. In the winter, all adults have an entirely snow-white plumage with only the bill remaining black.

NESTING AND REPRODUCTION

The reproduction of all species of ptarmigan is similar, and of all species of grouse only the ptarmigan is monogamous. A male begins his courtship and pairing in late April or early May in northwestern North America (in April in the Canadian arctic) and battles savagely with other males to win and keep his spouse. The male does not engage in fantastic courtship displays but does call loud and frequently during the midnight hours. His calls are a series of hoarse squeaks and croaks.

Each hen builds a depression in the ground, lines it with leaves and grass, and then lays seven to twelve eggs. The color of the egg varies from pale yellow to chestnut-brown, and is heavily spotted with deep brown and black. The incubation period is twenty-one to twenty-two days, with renesting occurring only rarely. Most hens in a given area nest at the same time. Hatching peaks are from June 20 to July 5 in subarctic and alpine tundras and in late July in the Canadian arctic. Male ptarmigan accompany the hen and chicks until the youngsters are full grown. Young ptarmigan are able to fly about ten days after hatching.

It is well known that there is a great variation in abundance of ptarmigan from year to year. Why this is so is not completely known. Some believe the ptarmigan reach peaks of abundance every nine or ten years, but convincing evidence of cycles is lacking.

FEEDING PATTERNS AND HABITS

From June to August, ptarmigan eat a wide variety of plant foods, herbs, insects, snails, and berries. Blueberries, huckleberries, cranberries, moss-berries, and seeds are an important part of the fall diet. Then in winter the birds switch to rock moss, lichens, willow buds, dwarf alders, dwarf birch buds, and needles. The spring diet consists of dried berries, new green leaves, and stems. Because the white-tailed ptarmigan lives mostly above the timber line, it is more inclined to feed on mossberries and lichens than on tree buds.

LOCATING HUNTING AREAS

Late summer and autumn are times of increasing gregariousness, movement, and sex segregation. Flock formation occurs in August and September and is variable in size. Groups of 20 to 200 are common. Partial separation of sexes in winter is common among ptarmigan; each flock is almost entirely composed of members of the same sex.

Autumn movement and migration to the wintering grounds is typical of ptarmigan. Some movements are extensive, as much as 500 miles. Willow and rock ptarmigan drop down to more southerly latitudes. The willow ptarmigan seeks the shelter of willow groves for winter; the rock ptarmigan, which frequents the highest and most barren slopes in the summer, drops down to the more sheltered slopes. The white-tailed ptarmigan migrates less and spends both summer and winter in the bleak alpine heights of the mountains.

White-tailed ptarmigan are the most difficult to hunt since they occupy mountain slopes high above timber line. Climbing to reach them is rugged work. Once reached, however, they are easy to approach; when flushed, they fly only a short distance and try to escape by running among rocks.

Early in the season, rock and willow ptarmigan are found in small flocks on barrens and tundra. When in cover they will lie to a dog; otherwise they tend to run and must be chased down and made to flush. Later in the season, when they assemble in large flocks, they flush wilder and are hard for pointing dogs to handle. When in the lowlands of willows, alders, birch, and other cover, they can be routed out by good flushing dogs, or by parties of hunters tramping the cover.

HUNTING METHODS

The ptarmigan is unique among the birds of North America in that more are taken annually for food than for recreation. The season in Alaska extends from August 20 to April 15, with some exceptions. This allows the villagers ample opportunity to kill the ptarmigan for food. It has been reported, for example, that 422 hunters in eleven villages along the northwest coast took 29,464 ptarmigan in a recent year. There is no indication that populations are being affected by this wide-scale hunting. Lack of access to much ptarmigan country limits the harvesting of these birds. As populations in Alaska and other northern regions continues to increase, however, and as the number of hunters increases, the harvest of ptarmigan could become excessive unless drastic curtailment of the season and bag limit occurs. The daily bag limit in Alaska is still twenty birds, with the season open for 258 days out of the year.

Ptarmigan are easy to approach and to hit when jumped. A dog is not necessary, although the birds will lie tight to a pointing dog. They are easiest to hunt when they are in large flocks and have moved to the lower elevations and latitudes for the winter. In provinces of Canada from Quebec to Saskatchewan, the harvest is entirely of migrant birds that have moved southward for winter. Usually the birds appear during November or December. Some ptarmigan are taken in the fall in the mountainous country of Alberta, British Columbia, and the Yukon Territory.

The peak hunting periods in Alaska are in August and September when the season opens for other species of game, and in February and March when improving weather, lengthening daylight, closed seasons on big game, and concentrations of ptarmigan close to roads attract hunters.

Data obtained at a checking station in central Alaska during August and September of one year revealed an average of about ten birds were in the possession of hunting parties when checked. Another year, the average in possession per party was about six birds. Populations of birds were up during the more successful year.

White-tailed ptarmigan in winter dress is not an easy bird to see, as he is well camouflaged against the snow. *Colo. Game and Fish Dept.*

9

Chukar and Hungarian Partridge

CHUKAR PARTRIDGE—IDENTIFICATION

THE CHUKAR partridge (*Alectoris graeca*) is also called red-legged partridge (Europe), Barbary partridge, chukar, Indian chukar, chickore, chuckare, and chukru. In size, it is approximately 12-14 inches long and weighs about 1¼ pounds, midway between the common bobwhite and the ruffed grouse. Females are slightly smaller, weighing about 18 ounces.

The chukar is distinctly marked and easily recognizable. Most prominent is the narrow black band which begins above the bill and follows the cheeks across the eyes, passes down the side of the neck and across the upper breast encircling the throat. Black bars are especially noticeable along the cream-colored sides and flanks. The throat and cheek varies from white to tan. The top of the head, neck, and across the back is slate-gray and buff or reddish-brown. The tail is ash-gray with the outer feathers reddish. The bill, legs, and feet are red. Males usually have slightly larger spur-like knobs on the leg. The colors and markings on both sexes are similar.

RANGE AND DISTRIBUTION

Chukars are not native to the United States but were introduced into this country (into Illinois) from northern India in 1893. Various species and subspecies are found in Mongolia, Tibet, India, Arabia, Egypt, Asia Minor, and southern Europe. These early introductions were not successful; the first successful plants were made in California. Then in 1935 some sportsmen in Nevada decided to try the bird among the arid, barren slopes of that state. This kind of country was to the bird's liking. Nevada held the first unlimited hunt for the birds in the United States in 1947. In 1958 hunters bagged a record 115,000 birds. The total harvest in Nevada since the first plantings has been over 500,000 birds. After Nevada's success, other states, namely Washington, Oregon, Idaho, California, Montana, Hawaii, Utah, Wyoming, and

137

The proud chukar partridge stands poised, strikingly marked by a narrow black band which stretches across its eyes and ends in a V on its throat. *Oregon Game Commission*

Distribution of the chukar partridge

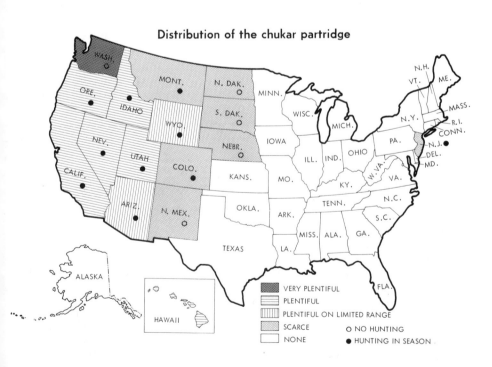

Colorado held hunts. The bird is now found in nineteen states; twelve of these states have open season on the bird. However, in western states with suitable habitat, the chukar partridge is still spreading, and promises to be an even more important game bird in the future.

NESTING AND REPRODUCTION

Chukars pair off at various times depending on the climate of the state. For example, pairing off takes place in Washington around the first of February; in Oregon and Utah, about mid-March; in Nevada, toward the end of March; and in Minnesota, in early April. The chukar is usually monogamous, and each pair goes off by itself to court and nest. Occasionally, however, one male mates with two females. Nesting usually begins about three weeks after pairing. The nest is made on the ground under lowstanding shrubs, clumps of grass, or other vegetation, and consists only of a hollowed place lined with coarse, dried grasses. From ten to twenty-two brownish-speckled eggs are laid with the average being fifteen. If one nest is destroyed, the chukar will renest. Incubation takes about twenty-four days during which time the male remains nearby. The males do not, however, assist in the care of the young. On the average, about twelve out of fifteen eggs will hatch, are cared for by the hen, and usually band together with other broods near water holes during the summer months.

FEEDING PATTERNS AND HABITS

Chukars eat grass and weed seeds, green sprouts, leaves and flowers, waste grain, and wild fruits. Insects are consumed during the summer. Chukars need not depend upon agricultural production for food, since they can forage for themselves as long as natural food is present. If, however, their food supply is covered by snow, many birds starve. This is one reason why chukars do not thrive in areas of heavy snow. The bird is a ground feeder and does not eat tree buds as do grouse. Thus, all its food must come from bare ground or from weed stalks sticking up through the snow. Chukars have been observed eating ragweed, dock, and evening primrose seeds.

LOCATING HUNTING AREAS

Why chukars will not establish themselves in rich agricultural areas where food would be more plentiful is not clearly understood. They prefer semi-arid country, and trying to raise them in the corn belt of the Midwest is like trying to raise caribou on the streets of New York.

They like areas of low shrubs or rocky outcrops which provide loafing or escape cover on steep barren hillsides. In Nevada, for example, chukars inhabit the rocky barren cheat-grass ridges in the open mountain and hill country, where elevations reach 4,000 to 10,000 feet. Since the birds need water holes, especially during the hot dry summer months, they often con-

These chukars search desperately for food under the snow in the Badlands of South Dakota. The bird lives on natural food, and heavy snow can cut off its supply. *North Dakota State Game and Fish Dept.*

gregate in areas where water is readily available. During the wet spring, fall or winter, however, they may be found far from water holes.

Studies of chukar populations reveal that the numbers of birds fluctuate with range conditions. When yearly moisture and other factors provide for a good feed year, the birds become abundant. During drought years, they diminish. Wet and drought years occur more or less in cycles and the fluctuation of these birds generally follows these cycles.

HUNTING METHODS

Chukars are fast on the wing and offer no easy target. They often try to run before flushing, always uphill. Large coveys in particular will scatter and run up the side of a ridge rather than flush. Or, if they do flush, they often flush wild and then always fly downhill for some distance. After scattering, a good pointing dog is a help in finding small groups or singles, which lie fairly well to the dog. But when the large coveys are in open country, pointing dogs are useless.

It is hard to specify the best time to hunt chukars. During rainy weather chukars are hard to find since they do not have to visit water holes. During dry hot weather, they may come to water anytime from early morning to evening, though chances of finding them near water are better early and late in the day.

Hunting chukars is easier if coveys are located first. They can be seen running across roads near creeks, or they can be heard calling to one another with their familiar "chuck,chuck,chuckarr,chuckarr" call. After flushing, chukars generally call "chie-u,chie-u" which helps to locate singles and small groups.

Once located, the problem is to get the covey to flush within range. When coveys are located on the side of steep ridges above a hunter, a retriever can be sent ahead to flush the birds. They will fly downhill toward the hunter. A few hunters without dogs, chasing chukars uphill, will find the birds always just out of range, impossible to catch or flush. In flat country, however, a man can run the birds down and make them flush.

If the hunter can get above hillside coveys, the birds flush easily since their escape route uphill is cut off. Or, if a group of hunters work a ridge, some men on top and some on the bottom of the slope, the uphill hunters flush birds which fly downhill, and the downhill hunters chase birds, which run uphill. The best system with a group, therefore, is to move along the side (not up or down) of a ridge with some hunters top and some bottom. This way the hunters can keep the partridge moving up and down within range.

HUNGARIAN PARTRIDGE

Other common names for the Hungarian partridge (*Perdix perdix*) are hun, gray partridge (Europe), European partridge, and European gray partridge.

IDENTIFICATION

This bird is 12 to 14 inches long and weighs 12 to 13 ounces. The color is grayish and rusty-brown, barred with chestnut on the sides, lower breast and flanks, with fine lines of gray, brown, and black found throughout the feather pattern. The gray on the breast and shoulders is a soft pastel tone, similar to that on the dove, while the gray on the back has more brown. The wings are brown with white lines running lengthwise through them. On the female, these light stripes are crossbarred. Adult males have a prominent chestnut colored horseshoe marking on the breast. The face and throat are chestnut colored.

RANGE AND DISTRIBUTION

The Hungarian partridge originated in Central Europe. These birds are found in numbers on the great agricultural plains of Hungary, hence the term "Hungarian." The first plantings were in 1899, when about two dozen birds were placed on a private preserve in Virginia. A little later another planting was made; by 1906, more than 180 birds had been released, but they quickly disappeared. In 1900, nearly 100 birds were liberated in the Willamette Valley, Oregon, and by 1906 about 5,000 had been released in Washington. From these plantings, the range spread from Washington and Oregon into Idaho, Montana, and parts of British Columbia.

The biggest boom in huns occurred, however, when Alberta released over 500 birds in 1908 and 1909. The results were phenomenal. The birds spread throughout Alberta, to Manitoba and Saskatchewan and down through the border states of the Dakotas, Montana, Idaho, and Oregon.

Most plantings in the East ended in failure. Birds planted in South Carolina, North Carolina, Massachusetts, Virginia, New York, New Jersey, Pennsylvania, and Mississippi disappeared, sometimes after a brief period of success. Some plantings in the Midwest were moderately successful. Generally,

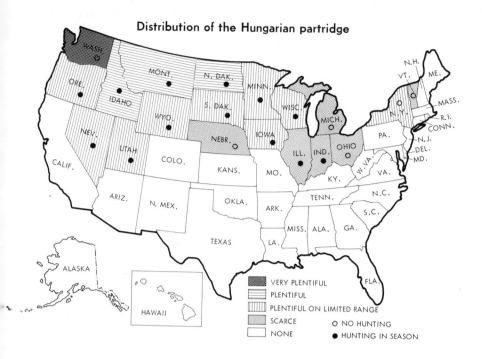

Distribution of the Hungarian partridge

Legend:
- VERY PLENTIFUL
- PLENTIFUL
- PLENTIFUL ON LIMITED RANGE
- SCARCE
- NONE
- O NO HUNTING
- ● HUNTING IN SEASON

however, the hun continues to thrive in the prairie provinces of Canada and the Northern states west of the Great Lakes. The bird can stand rugged winters where food is plentiful, so it thrives in fertile farmlands, particularly in the grain belts of North America. As can be seen by the map, the bird is now found in nineteen states and is hunted in sixteen of these.

NESTING AND REPRODUCTION

Huns begin to pair off in late January, February, or early March, depending upon the locality and the weather. If the weather becomes severe, each pair may join with others to form large coveys until the cold spell is gone.

Hungarian partridge enclosed and hidden by the thick grassland it prefers as a habitat during the spring and summer. *South Dakota Dept. of Game, Fish and Parks.*

Nesting begins in late April or early May. The cock is monogamous by choice and a devoted parent and mate. During mating time he is pugnacious and will guard his own territory against all intruders. The number of eggs laid varies from ten to twenty, with the average about sixteen olive-white eggs laid at the the rate of about two every three days. The nest is usually a well-concealed depression in alfalfa stubble, wasteland, or grassy fence rows and is lined with dried grass and feathers. The male does not help in the incubation, which takes twenty-three to twenty-four days, but does help in the care of the young. When danger threatens, both adults scold and feign to draw off intruders. The alarm note is sharp and metallic, accompanied by a flaunting of the tail feathers.

The Hungarian partridge nesting below protective grassland. The birds guard their nests fiercely from all intruders. *North Dakota State Game and Fish Dept.*

FEEDING PATTERNS AND HABITS

The young feed mostly on ants and ant pupae. During their growth period, young huns relish locusts, grasshoppers, crickets, potato bugs, and other insects. All huns relish green plant food as a part of the diet all year round. Weed and grass seeds and waste grain are important foods during the summer. For this reason, these birds are found almost exclusively in grasslands and stubble fields at this time of the year. During the winter, huns try to work down through the snow in search of sprouted winter grain. As long as food is available, the birds remain on the open prairies all winter; otherwise they move to heavier cover where they live on tree buds and other foods above the snow.

HUNTING METHODS

The Hungarian partridge is a challenge to the hunter, with or without a dog. Huns are very fast on the wing. When flushed, a covey explodes with rapid wing beats as it alternately glides and flies away. The covey does stay grouped, however, and most members land together in an adjoining field. Since the covey usually does not fly far, it can often be located and flushed again.

Partridge are masters at camouflage and sulking, however. Many times I have walked up to a covey which I have seen fly onto an open, plowed field, but have not been able to see the birds, even on the bare ground, until they flushed.

At other times, huns that are spotted will not let you get close enough for a shot before flushing. This is especially true in open country. Most of the time, however, I have been able to sneak up on a spotted covey.

LOCATING HUNTING AREAS

The principal problem is locating the birds. Most coveys are widely scattered. Remember that huns are more active early and late in the day and can often be spotted by the careful observer of nearby fields while road hunting for other species.

A party of hunters without dogs can line up and tramp through pastures, grain and hayfields, particularly near cultivated farm land where there is a lot of waste grain, with good results. I generally prefer to hunt along the edges of fields, small patches of cover, and fencerows.

A fast far-ranging pointer who comes on a covey suddenly can pin the birds down until the hunter arrives. A slow creeping animal makes the birds run ahead and around, though generally huns do not try to escape by running. I use my labrador retriever as a flushing dog with some success, particularly in fairly heavy cover.

If some individual birds are separated from a covey after flushing, they do considerable calling and can be located by their sound.

10

Woodcock and Jacksnipe

BECAUSE OF the close relationship between the woodcock and the jacksnipe, or Wilson's snipe, they will be treated together. Neither the woodcock nor the jacksnipe is hunted as heavily as many of our other game birds, partly because of their small size, and partly because of the exceedingly heavy cover which these birds often inhabit. Both species, however, provide wonderful sport for the skilled shotgunner, are very good eating, and are plentiful and easy to locate.

IDENTIFICATION–WOODCOCK

The woodcock (*Philohela minor*) is quite an interesting looking bird. The size of its long needle-like bill in relation to the rest of its body is disproportionate. This gives the bird a rather awkward appearance, but it is very swift and agile in flight. Woodcock average about 11 inches in length, are generally brown in coloration with dark blackish-brown markings covering the entire back, much of the sides, and the top of the head. The underparts blend to a lighter tan with a cast of orange or peach, and the tail, wings, and forehead just in front of the eyes and above the bill are a light tannish-gray. The legs, compared to those of the jacksnipe, are quite short, and of dull pink coloration. The body of the woodcock is very plump, the neck short, and the head rather large. The eyes are large, and of dark brownish-black coloration. The male and female of this species are similar in all respects except size; the female is slightly the larger of the two. Because of regional variation in the size of these birds, the sexes can be determined only by dissection.

The woodcock in flight is exciting to watch; it is swift, erratic, and makes a combination of chafing and whistling sounds which are loud enough to be heard at considerable distances. The wing strokes are rapid and powerful, giving the woodcock great speed and maneuverability. When flushed the woodcock springs almost vertically from its hiding place, levels off abruptly, and is gone in a few seconds.

RANGE AND DISTRIBUTION

As seen by the map, the woodcock is found in thirty-seven states and hunted in thirty-four of these. It is fairly plentiful throughout the eastern half of the United States, particularly east of the Mississippi River in the more heavily wooded sections. It breeds from northeastern North Dakota, southern Manitoba, Michigan, southern Quebec and Nova Scotia, south to Kansas, Louisiana, and Florida. It winters from the Ohio Valley to New Jersey, then angles south to Texas. The woodcock is a migratory bird, but little is known about its paths of migration, and it disappears suddenly from some areas along its route south. The explanation of this mystery is found in the nocturnal flying habits of this species.

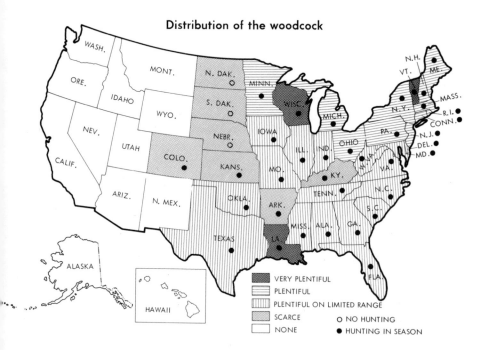

Distribution of the woodcock

NESTING AND REPRODUCTION

Like many other game birds, the woodcock has an interesting and elaborate mating ritual. The male selects his breeding site, fluffs his feathers and struts back and forth, uttering a repeated nasal call in an attempt to attract a mate. Every few minutes, the cock will take off and climb in spiral ascent to a height of 300 feet. He then punges in an erratic, gyrating dive to the earth, alights, and repeats the strutting pattern over again.

As a rule, only one nesting occurs each season, and this usually provides an adequate number of new birds to replace those lost to hunters and natural predation during the previous year. The nest is always constructed of dry leaves, grass, and twigs on the ground, usually in a densely brushy area near the water. The nest is well concealed, sometimes under roots or other debris, and its material and undisciplined manner of construction constitute a kind of camouflage in themselves. Usually the eggs are laid early in May, though they may come earlier if the weather is good. The hen lays four eggs of light pinkish-tan, with darker reddish-brown markings over the entire surface. It takes about twenty-one days for the eggs to incubate, and the hen sticks very close to her nest during this period.

It is not known if the male aids in the incubation of the eggs. It is impossible to tell if a male or female is sitting on a nest. The hen will allow an extremely close approach while sitting on her eggs if she feels she is not seen. At other times she will affect the broken wing trick so common to many of our ground-nesting birds.

The young of the woodcock are precocious and move from the nest almost as soon as they are hatched. For the first few weeks they are closely guarded by the hen, but begin their first flights at about two weeks of age. They are completely independent at four weeks. By the time a woodcock is six months old it is fully grown and mature in every respect. It takes time to develop the tremendous pectoral muscles of the adult bird, however, and the young never exhibit the strength and agility in flight common to their elders. Because of their excellent means of concealment, and their elusive habits of nocturnal feeding and flight, it is difficult to gauge the population or the survival rates of these birds. We can only say that there are good and bad woodcock years.

FEEDING PATTERNS AND HABITS

Woodcocks feed almost entirely on one kind of earthworm, the common angleworm, using the long, sensitive bill in conjunction with extremely acute hearing. Much like the robin, the woodcock walks along on the soft earth and mud flats that harbor the angleworm, tilting its head from side to side listening for worms, and then plunges its bill into the soft earth to spear a worm. The tip of the upper mandible has a tiny flexible tip which is reputed to have super-sensitivity, and may aid the bird in locating worms beneath the surface of the earth.

The woodcock is a nocturnal feeder as well as flyer, and it is extremely unusual to see one feeding. In general the feeding grounds of the woodcock will be found fairly close to water, as the ground must be soft and damp both to allow insertion of his bill, and to attract the earthworm. Low-lying, leaf-covered boggy areas in woods and thickets, near streams and sloughs, provide the best feeding habitat for this bird.

LOCATING HUNTING AREAS

When looking for places to hunt woodcock, it is best to confine yourself to the feeding areas. Slough bottoms, surrounded by brushy undergrowth, alder, willow, and other marshy woods, are especially good; similar growth along rivers and lake shores can be equally productive. However, the wood-cock, like the mourning dove, does not always stay in the same areas, and there are many excellent appearing covers which rarely hold a bird.

Feeding areas of the woodcock can be easily located during the daytime by looking at the surface of the mudflats where you suspect they have been. If the mud is covered with small holes, and also with white droppings, you can be reasonably sure that they have been in the area. Along the migration routes, however, the stay of the woodcock is often brief; sometimes they will stay a few hours, sometimes several days. At any rate, after you find them you must hunt them quickly, before they are gone. It does little good, unless you are totally unfamiliar with your area, to do much pre-season looking for hunting spots. Frequently a thicket near an out-of-the-way pothole, perhaps deep in the woods, provides good shooting year after year, and the more places of this kind that you can add to your collection the better. With the proper approach and acute observation, you are likely to discover a number of these good woodcock covers.

It is important to bear in mind that the woodcock has evolved toward an adaptation to upland habitat. This is evidenced in its short legs, heavy body, and its instinct to hold tight, even for a pointing dog. You can take advantage of this by finding hunting locations, especially brush-covered hillsides and small swales not too distant from the prime feeding grounds. If there are woodcock in the area, a certain number of them will roost in this kind of cover during the day. This provides not quite as many shots as the heavier wetter thickets of the lowlands, but somewhat more pleasant shooting con-ditions.

HUNTING METHODS

Hunting woodcock, once they have been located, is a simple procedure. If the birds are roosting and sitting very tightly, it is the hunter's job to put them into the air. This can be done by walking them up. However, with a bird that sits as closely as the woodcock it is an advantage to use a pointing dog. For this type of hunting, the pointer or setter must be a close worker, as a wide ranger would be out of sight and hearing in the dense covers, and hence of little value. It is also a good idea to attach a loud bell to the collar of your dog so that you will know when and where he has struck a point. You must realize, however, that there are very few good woodcock dogs. This is because so few dogs have a good enough nose to work a bird which sits so tightly and gives off so little scent.

In all cases, woodcock covers should be slowly and carefully worked, whether you are hunting the ridges and hillside thickets or heavy brush near the water's edge. The element of surprise is tremendous as the birds explode from beneath your feet, particularly if you are not using a pointer. In addition

The most effective way to hunt woodcock is to walk them up, causing them to flush. This hunter uses a pointer to help him locate the covey. *Michigan Conservation Dept.*

Two hunters and their dog contemplate their woodcock. A good day's hunting ends up at this rushing stream. *Michigan Conservation Dept.*

their extremely rapid acceleration after they have been frightened by a shot makes them an exceedingly difficult target to hit.

IDENTIFICATION—JACKSNIPE

The jacksnipe (*Capella gallinago delicata*) is slightly longer than the woodcock, averaging about 12 inches in length, but with a smaller breast. In coloration the snipe is pale brown fading to tannish-white on the breast, and is mottled with dark brown to blackish-brown running in two longitudinal bars down the head and back, with mottled feathers on either side. The feathers on the shoulders have a white edging which gives the effect of a white strip on either side of the bird. The bill, like that of the woodcock, is very long and narrow, and the upper mandible extends over the lower. The color of the bill is a dull flesh blending to dark, almost black, on the tip of the upper mandible. The legs are somewhat longer than those of the woodcock, and the jacksnipe moves more freely on them; they are grayish green in color. Like its cousin, the woodcock, the sexes are practically indistinguishable in the jacksnipe, and they can be positively identified only by dissection.

The snipe is also an extremely fast and often erratic flyer; in fact, the ones that I have observed gave the impression of greater speed and maneuverability than the woodcock. The flight silhouettes and patterns between the two birds, however, are similar. The jacksnipe produces a strange and sometimes startling rushing sound in flight similar to that of the woodcock.

The jacksnipe, recognized by its prominent bill and white edging on its shoulder feathers, flies very fast and offers good shotgunning to the hunter. *Michigan Conservation Dept.*

RANGE AND DISTRIBUTION

The jacksnipe is much more widespread than the woodcock, and is found in forty-six states; forty-four of these allow hunting. It is known on both coasts as well as inland. Its breeding grounds extend from Alaska through much of Canada to northern California, across to Iowa, and from there to New Jersey. It winters from northern California through Arizona, New Mexico, Oklahoma, Arkansas, Tennessee, and North Carolina, through Central America, the West Indies, and as far south as Colombia and Brazil. The jacksnipe migrates in much the same fashion and general flyways as the ducks and geese which breed in the same areas, but the snipe is less hardy than the ducks, and its migration starts earlier in the season.

NESTING AND REPRODUCTION

The jacksnipe goes through a mating ritual similar to that of the wood-

Distribution of the jacksnipe

VERY PLENTIFUL
PLENTIFUL
PLENTIFUL ON LIMITED RANGE
SCARCE   O NO HUNTING
NONE   ● HUNTING IN SEASON

cock. He selects his mating ground, and then flies high into the air, moving in wide circles. He then plummets to earth, struts about, and repeats the soaring performance. These antics usually occur in early morning and late evening, though they occasionally court on moonlit nights. In most areas, the jacksnipe nests later than the woodcock, usually late May or early June. The nest is a grass-lined depression in marshy ground and is not so well concealed as that of the woodcock. The eggs of the jacksnipe number three or four, are olive-green in color, and are mottled and streaked with brown and black. Like those of its cousin, the young of the jacksnipes mature rapidly, grow fast, learn to fly quickly, and generally become independent while very young.

FEEDING PATTERNS AND HABITS

The jacksnipe, like the woodcock, depends on the use of its long pointed bill, and the presence of soft earth containing earthworms and larva for its food. However, the snipe eats other forms of insect and worm life which the woodcock would not normally eat. Various larva, crustaceans, earthworms, grasshoppers and locusts comprise the bulk of their diet. Although the jacksnipe is not as strictly nocturnal as the woodcock, most of its feeding and flying activity takes place at dusk, dawn, and during the night. I have seen the largest numbers of these birds late in the afternoons, just before sunset, when they come in to the slough bottoms to feed. The jacksnipe must have wet ground for its feeding activities and is probably more dependent on actual slough and marshland than the woodcock. For this reason, maintenance of water levels is an important factor in keeping these birds in any area.

LOCATING HUNTING AREAS

Jacksnipe can often be found in the same areas as woodcock, though they rarely roost as far upland as the latter. The best cover for jacksnipe is the shallow grassy slough with intermittent muddy flats. These areas, if they are not to boggy or deep, and have comparatively short grass cover, are very easily hunted. Good jacksnipe locations can often be found when looking for duck hunting areas, and I have never found them quite so unpredictable in their habitat as woodcock. This is partly because of the woodcock's habit of seeking out the seclusion of deep woodland potholes. Snipe roost in the thickets too, but usually much closer to their feeding grounds in the sloughs.

HUNTING METHODS

There are two basic ways to hunt jacksnipe: one is effective at almost any time of day, if the right areas are hunted; and the other is reserved for late afternoon and early morning shooting. Probably the most common method of hunting these birds is simply to "walk them up" in the manner of woodcock hunting. Dogs are not commonly used in hunting jacksnipe, and I have never heard of the use of a pointer. A well-controlled, close-working flushing dog could be of use in this sport, but I have never found that the snipe sat so tightly that a dog was needed to flush them. It is an excellent idea, however, to have a good retriever along at heel, as these birds are extremely difficult to find in the heavy slough cover once they are downed because of their protective coloration. I have had good results hunting jacksnipe in this manner with no other equipment than my gun, a few shells, and a pair of hip boots.

The alternate method of hunting snipe is to wait in a blind or to crouch in the grass near a known feeding area and wait for them to come in. This must be done either very early in the morning, or just before sunset as they do not move about much at any other time of day. Snipe decoys have been used in the past, and while they are rarely seen today, they may be of use stuck here and there in the mud to attract the birds. I have never observed strong gregarious behavior among jacksnipe or woodcock, however, and these birds never respond to decoys to the extent that ducks and geese do. I have never found jacksnipe to be particularly wary, and often they will fly over within easy gun range as you walk through a slough or along a shore.

Both woodcock and jacksnipe offer sport in a substantial part of the United States and Canada. Very little equipment is needed to hunt them, and long expensive trips in their quest are not necessary. An extra attraction is their delectable presence on the table. They are hard to surpass in their sporting qualities, as, along with the mourning dove, they offer some of the most challenging shooting that can be had.

11

Shotguns, Loads and Wing Shooting

WHAT GUN?

There are five things to consider when selecting a shotgun:

1. What gauge or bore is best for the type of hunting you do?

2. What degree of choke will give the best pattern at the most probable ranges?

3. How long should the barrel be?

4. What actions suit you the best? Should you buy a single-shot break action, side-by-side double, over-and-under double, bolt action, pump, or autoloader?

5. Does the gun fit you?

Shotguns made in the United States come in 6 gauges, or bore diameters. The following table shows the bore diameter in inches for each of the six gauges.

Gauge	.410	28	20	16	12	10
Bore Diameter	.410	.550	.615	.670	.730	.775

Obviously, the larger the bore the larger the shotgun shell that can be used, and the more powder and pellets the shell can contain. If maximum killing power were the only consideration in selecting the gauge of a shotgun, the 10-gauge gun would always be used. However, it is possible to be over-gunned, especially when hunting the smaller birds like dove or quail. Other factors also must be considered: the weight of a gun, its balance and ease in handling, the ability with which the hunter can aim and shoot it accurately, the recoil power and effect on the hunter, the ease with which the gun can be loaded, the safety in handling it, and so forth.

The lightest gun is the .410, but it is so small that its range and killing power are severely limited. The most powerful gun is the 10 gauge, but this is so heavy and recoil is so great, as to make it very unpleasant to use. Selection of the gauge is inevitably a compromise between maximum range and killing power and minimum weight and ease of handling.

The following table shows the average quantity of shot of various sizes found in different weights of shot loads.

Gauge	Length of Shell in Inches	Ounces of Shot	Number of Pellets Shot Sizes				
			7½	6	5	4	2
.410	2½	½	175	112	85	67	45
.410	3	¾	262	169	127	101	67
28	2¾	¾	262	169	127	101	67
20	2¾	⅞	306	197	149	118	79
28	2¾ Mag.	1	350	225	170	135	90
20	2¾	1	350	225	170	135	90
16	2¾	1	350	225	170	135	90
12	2¾	1	350	225	170	135	90
20	2¾ Mag.	1⅛	394	253	191	152	101
16	2¾	1⅛	394	253	191	152	101
12	2¾	1⅛	394	253	191	152	101
20	3 Mag.	1¼	437	281	212	169	112
16	2¾ Mag.	1¼	437	281	212	169	112
12	2¾	1¼	437	281	212	169	112
12	3 Mag.	1⅜	480	310	234	186	124
12	2¾ Mag.	1½	525	337	255	202	135
12	3 Mag.	1⅝	570	366	276	220	146
10	2⅞	1⅝	570	366	276	220	146
12	3 Mag.	1⅞	656	422	319	253	169
10	3½ Mag.	2	700	450	340	270	180

Loads of 1, 1⅛, and 1¼ ounces of shot can be purchased in any one of the three most common gauges: 20 gauge, 16 gauge, and 12 gauge. Since loads below 1 ounce of shot are too light for most birds, I would therefore eliminate from all consideration the .410 gauge. The .410 is alright for rats, doves, or sparrows, but not for rugged and heavily feathered ducks or geese. This gun will cripple many birds, even doves and quail, so it is really not a sporting gun. The most sportsmanlike gun is actually the one which kills keenly and quickly at reasonable ranges without mutilating the bird.

Also, I would eliminate the 28 gauge in standard loads of ¾ ounces. Even in the 2¾-inch magnum load with 1 ounce of shot, the gunner only comes up to the bare minimum for the larger birds. For some types of pass shooting requiring reasonably far ranges, this gun is still inadequate. It is a popular gun in Europe for upland game, and is a favorite among women and small boys, but the serious hunter ought to bypass it for most waterfowl and upland game hunting.

The 20-gauge gun is a marvelously light gun, easy to handle and point, and is very fast-shooting. This gun is perfectly adequate in light field loads for smaller birds. In the express loads with 1 ounce of shot, you are under-gunned for some types of larger bird hunting, so use the 2¾-inch or 3-inch magnum loads, when long-range shooting is required. For maximum range in this gauge use the 3-inch magnum load. The 20-gauge gun which is cham-bered to take 3-inch magnum shells is the lightest gun you can use and still have enough power and 1¼ ounces of shot. This is really equivalent in shot charge to shooting express loads in a 12-gauge gun.

As far as I can see, there is no real reason to buy a 16-gauge gun. You can use shells for it containing either 1, 1⅛ or 1¼ ounces of shot. It is not made in the 3-inch magnum size, so you can get no more power or range from it than from the 3-inch magnum 20 gauge. My advice is either to buy a 20 or a 12, not a 16.

The 12-gauge gun has always been the standard all-around weapon. The real advantage is that you can use such a wide variety of shells and loads. The 12 gauge field loads have only 1 ounce of shot; the 3 inch magnum shell holds 1⅞ ounces. All sizes in between can also be used. When equipped with a variable-choke device, or when barrels with different chokes are used, the 12 gauge becomes the most versatile weapon. It can be used on quail, doves, and other small upland game, and on ducks and geese as well.

I would strongly advise against buying a 10-gauge shotgun. To be sure, you can kill ducks and geese with it at a range of 60–70 yards, but most hunters can't hit moving waterfowl at much over 40 yards anyhow. Beyond that range, it is very difficult to judge the amount of lead needed to hit the target. So why be overgunned? A 10-gauge gun is murderous on the shoulder and a tiring weapon to hold and to carry. Also, the shells are expensive.

THE CHOKE

Choke is the constriction on the end of the barrel which keeps the shot from scattering and assures a fairly tight pattern of shot at medium to far ranges. Full choke gives the maximum constriction and the tightest pattern, and is therefore most effective at long ranges. Open choke or open cylinder means no constriction of the barrel, and therefore provides the maximum spread of shot. Open cylinder is appropriate only for close-range shooting. There are degrees of choke between full and open choke. There is also re-verse cylinder which opens the barrel up even more than open cylinder, and a full, full choke which gives a tighter pattern than the full choke.

The most common chokes are found in the following table. Pattern per-centage is the per cent of the total shot which is found within a 30-inch circle at 40 yards.

Choke	*Pattern Percentage*
Full	65-75
Improved Modified ($\frac{3}{4}$ choke)	55-65
Modified ($\frac{1}{2}$ choke)	45-55
Improved Cylinder ($\frac{1}{4}$ choke)	35-45
Cylinder	25-35

Every new gun is classified according to its degree of choke. However the designations are not always accurate, and sometimes refer to only certain sizes of shot. For example, a gun marked full choke may be true for number 4 shot, but have only modified choke with number 6 shot.

Therefore, test the pattern of your gun (before you buy it if possible) and determine the choke you want. Shoot several patterns, using different shot sizes and charges for each round until you determine the choke you want and the size shot which gives the best pattern.

In calculating pattern, you have to know the total number of pellets in the shot charge you are using. Let us say you are using a shot load of $1\frac{1}{4}$ ounces of number 6 shot. As seen by the previous table, such a load would contain 281 pellets. To determine the pattern, measure off 40 yards from a piece of patterning paper or large piece of cardboard, fire a shot into the paper and then scribe a 30-inch circle around the part which encompasses the most holes. Then count the number of the shot holes within the 30-inch circle. If there were 160 pellets, the pattern would be 160 divided by 281 or 57 per cent, in the slightly improved modified category.

In general, modified choke is usually the best all-around choke for the average hunter and for most guns. With this choke you can kill all but the far-ranging birds and you can also use the gun for upland game. If you use a double-barrel gun, I would get one barrel improved-cylinder and the other either modified or full choke.

If you plan to use only one good gun, get one with a variable choke, so you can change the setting. Some guns are supplied with various choke tubes that can be placed over the end. You can also purchase interchangeable barrels. If you can afford several guns, then get them with different chokes.

THE BARREL

A barrel length of 26 inches to 28 inches is about right for most guns. Most 12-gauge guns come in lengths of from 26 to 30 inches with the 3-inch magnum sometimes 32.

Longer barrels were once believed to have a significant effect on shot velocity. Extensive tests have revealed, however, that while the longer barrel does afford increased velocity, the difference is not great. Specifically, tests indicate that the average loss in velocity is about $6\frac{1}{2}$ foot-seconds per inch reduction below the 30-inch barrel length.

If a hunter has a 22-inch barrel, and shoots at a crossing bird flying at a speed of 60 miles per hour and at a distance of 20 yards, he would have to increase his lead by only 5 inches over the man using a 30-inch barrel. Suffice it to say that 2 to 4 inches in barrel length makes little practical difference in shot velocity. In other respects, the shorter barrel gives a faster swinging, better balanced, lighter gun. I see no need in buying a shotgun with a barrel length over 28 inches no matter what the gauge. If long-range shooting is required, then greater choke can be used.

THE SIX BASIC SHOTGUNS

There are six basic types of shotguns: single-shot break action; side-by-side double barrel; over-and-under double barrel; bolt-action repeater; pump-action repeater; and autoloader.

The single-shot gun is light, easy to shoot, and inexpensive. The single barrel comes in either hammer or hammerless design and most are of the automatic extractor type. The obvious disadvantage to this gun is that you have only one chance at your target. Most models are made only in full choke, another decided disadvantage. In the special youth sizes, with shortened stock, modified choke, and 20 gauge, 26-inch barrel, the gun makes a nice gift for a young beginner.

Before the advent of the pump and autoloaders the side-by-side double barrel gun was very popular. It is less used today because most hunters object to the sighting plane and because the double-barrel is as expensive as a good pump.

An advantage of the double-barrel is that you can have two different chokes, thus enabling you to meet a variety of situations. With the double trigger, you can select the barrel you want to shoot first. Some guns have a single non-selective trigger which fires each barrel separately. Others have a single selective trigger which allows switching to the barrel you want to use first. These guns are usually quite expensive.

Some double-barrels have positive extractors in which both shells are lifted out about ½ inch when the gun is broken. Other guns have selective extractors in which each barrel has its own extractor. When one shell has been fired, the extractor of that barrel throws out the empty cartridge.

The over-and-under double barrel has gained in popularity in the United States. It has several advantages over the side-by-side gun. The over-and-under has only a single-barrel sighting plane, it has less recoil (the recoil is straight back, not to the side as in the double-barrel), it is an easier gun to handle, and it is neat in appearance. It is, however, a costly gun.

The bolt-action repeater is the least expensive of all the repeating shotguns. However, the reloading and refiring of this gun is a fairly slow process. The gunner must reach forward with his trigger hand to operate the bolt, then bring his trigger hand back in place, re-aim and fire. In some guns, the clip must be removed to be refilled. However, this gun is faster to reload than some singles or doubles.

The pump-action repeater is one of the most commonly used guns. It is lower in cost, lighter in weight, and almost as fast to reload and shoot as the autoloader. The pump-action repeater with a variable-choke device, or modified choke, is about as versatile a gun as you can buy.

The autoloader is a favorite gun of many hunters, primarily because ot its speed in firing. I have often knocked down a bird on the third shot while hunting companions with doubles or pump-actions have been limited to two shots. With the autoloader, one can continue firing while following through the proper sighting plane, and without disturbing the sight path by having to cock the gun after each shot.

The autoloader is expensive, heavy, and can be dangerous if not handled with caution. A beginner with an autoloader is a menace. He may forget that the gun fires and reloads as fast as he pulls the trigger.

SHELLS

Every shell that you buy is labeled according to gauge, drams of powder, ounces of shot, and shot size. A shell labeled No. 12, 3¾-1¼-6, is 12 gauge, has 3¾ drams of powder, and 1¼ ounces of shot of number 6 size.

The shell you buy is determined by the gauge of gun you use, the species of bird hunted, and the average distances over which you will shoot. In general, the more ounces of shot per shell, the denser the pattern when using a certain choke and a particular size shot at a prescribed distance. It is a real advantage to use shells with adequate loads of shot. This is true whether you hunt small birds such as quail or large birds such as pheasant.

If you shoot a 20 gauge, use shells with 1 ounce of shot for small birds at close ranges, and the heaviest loads (1¼ ounces of shot in 3-inch magnum shells) for large birds at all ranges.

If you shoot a 12-gauge gun, you have the maximum variety of loads. You can use the lighter field loads with 1 or 1⅛ ounces of shot for small or large birds at very close ranges. You can also use the heavier loads of 1¼ ounces if you are shooting large birds at medium to far ranges (35 to 55 yards).

Shot size is important since the larger the shot the farther its effective killing range. However, remember that killing power depends upon the number of pellets which hit the bird as well as the velocity and penetration. In fact, shocking power increases in direct ratio to the square of the number of pellets which hit, regardless of size. Thus, three pellets striking home have nine times the shocking power of one. From this point of view, it is an advantage to use small shot. If number 2 shot is used as a base, there are 50 per cent more number 4's than 2's in each ounce, 89 per cent more number 5's, 150 per cent more number 6's and 289 percent more number 7½'s. Using number 4 shot as a base, there are 26 percent more number 5's than 4's and 67 percent more number 6's than 4's. Since it is generally agreed that it takes four or five pellets to kill a large tough bird like a duck or pheasant, the hunter ought to use shot that will give a sufficient pattern density and still carry out to reasonable ranges with adequate penetration. Obviously, the larger the bird, the larger the shot can be and still get the required minimum of four or five pellets into the body.

With these facts in mind, what shot size should be used for each species of bird mentioned in this book? The following table offers some suggestions:

Bird	Average Weight	Average Max. Range	Average Shot Size
Doves	3 to 4 oz.	Under 35 yds.	9 to 7½
Woodcock	4 to 7 oz.	Under 35 yds.	9 to 7½
Jacksnipe	4 to 7 oz.	Under 35 yds.	9 to 7½
Bobwhite Quail	4 to 6 oz.	Under 35 yds.	9 to 7½
Valley or Calif. Quail	4 to 7 oz.	Up to 35 yds.	8 to 7½
Gambel's Quail	4 to 7 oz.	Up to 35 yds.	8 to 7½
Mearn's Quail	4 to 7 oz.	Up to 35 yds.	8 to 7½
Scaled Quail	7½ oz.	Under 40 yds.	8 to 7½
Mountain Quail	9 to 16 oz.	Under 40 yds.	8 to 7½
Hungarian Partridge	12 to 13 oz.	Under 40 yds.	8 to 7½
Ptarmigan	12 to 20 oz.	Under 40 yds.	7½ to 6
Franklin's & Spruce Grouse	12 to 24 oz.	Under 40 yds.	7½ to 6
Chukar Partridge	18 to 20 oz.	Under 40 yds.	7½ to 6
Small Ducks	12 to 21 oz.	Up to 40 yds.	7½ to 6
Ruffed Grouse	1 to 1¾ lb.	Up to 45 yds.	7½ to 6
Pinnated Grouse	1½ to 2 lbs.	Under 50 yds.	6 to 5
Sharp-tailed Grouse	2 lbs.	Under 50 yds.	6 to 5
Large Ducks	2 lbs. & over	Up to 50 yds.	6 to 4
Pheasants	2½ to 3 lbs.	Up to 50 yds.	6 to 4
Blue Grouse	Up to 4 lbs.	Under 55 yds.	5 to 4
Small Geese	5 lbs. 5 oz.	Up to 55 yds.	4 to 2
Sage Grouse	5 to 8 lbs.	Under 60 yds.	4 to 2
Large Canada Geese	8 lbs. 4 oz.	Up to 60 yds.	2 to BB

Maximum ranges depend upon the choke and pattern of a particular gun as much as on shot size, so each hunter ought to pattern his gun at various ranges with different shot sizes to determine the maximum effective range at which a good pattern can still be maintained.

WING SHOOTING

Successful wing shooting can be achieved if you use the right gun and shell; learn to hold and aim the gun, to lead your target and follow through correctly; and if you practice.

One of the important considerations is to get a gun that fits you. Several simple tests determine this.

First put your finger on the trigger and point the gun into the air until the gun butt rests in the crook of your elbow. The stock of the gun should be just long enough to fit into the hollow of your arm. Another way to test the pull is to put your gun to your shoulder as you would when raising the gun to fire. If the stock comes right to the shoulder without catching on your clothes, it it just the right length. If you have to pull the gun butt to your shoulder after the gun is in firing position, the pull is too short.

Most standard-size guns have a stock with a pull of 14 in. This is designed for the average man. Special youth sizes can also be obtained. These guns usually have a pull of 12½ in. If you require other than the standard or youth size, but can't afford a custom-built stock, you can alter the pull of your gun easily.

If the stock (or pull) is too short, add a rubber recoil pad. If the pull is too long, remove a pad already on or cut down the length of the stock.

Next, test the drop of the comb –the distance the comb is below the line of sight. Raise your gun to a normal shooting position, placing your cheek naturally and firmly against the comb. In this position, you should be looking right down the barrel at your target without having to raise or lower your head. When the comb is too high the shooter sees too much barrel, and raises the gun muzzle in compensation. As a consequence he shoots high. When the comb is too low, the shooter will try to raise it, thus lowering the gun muzzle. As a consequence he shoots too low. Improper comb height prevents the gunner from developing speed in his shooting, since he must constantly try to adjust his sighting plane.

Most shotguns have a drop at the comb of 1½ in. A few have more or less than this: 1¼ in., 1⅝ in. or 1⅚ in. Some youth models have a drop of 2¼ in. If your shotgun doesn't fit, alterations can be made at home or by a gunsmith.

If the comb of your gun is too high, it can be cut down carefully by an experienced cabinet maker or gunsmith. If you do the job yourself, work carefully, cutting off only a little at a time with a wood rasp and sandpaper.

If the comb of your gun is too low, it is a bit more of a problem, but the simplest way to correct it is to put on a laced leather sleeve, padded inside and at the top, which raises the comb height. If you object to the appearance of the sleeve, the wood can be built up, but the job is more expensive and requires an expert.

Test number three is used to determine the proper pitch of your gun. Pitch is the angle at which the butt plate is set in relation to the line of sight and it is measured at the muzzle of the gun. To determine if the pitch of your gun is correct, throw the gun to your shoulder as in normal shooting. If the pitch is just right, the gun will come to your shoulder and the butt will stick firmly there.

If the butt tends to slip down under the armpit, hasty shooting will tend to be high. If the butt tends to slip up, hasty shots will be thrown low. Thus, if both the pull and the drop at the comb seem right, but you are still shooting low, the pitch of your gun is too great and you need to take some off the heel of the stock. If the pull and drop are all right, but you are shooting high, the pitch is too small and you need to add to the heel or take off some of the toe of the stock. These alterations can be done at home or by a gunsmith.

If you need to decrease the pitch of your gun, the butt is cut off at the heel. If the pitch is to be increased, cut the butt off at the toe.

One other factor which determines the fit of your gun is the drop at the heel. No special test can be used to determine if it is correct, however, other than the general test of putting your gun to your shoulder. The fairly straight stock, one with but little more heel drop than comb drop, handles faster for most men who have done a lot of shooting, and such a stock has a mild kick. Most modern guns have a heel drop of $2\frac{1}{2}$ in. A few measure $2\frac{5}{16}$ in., $2\frac{3}{8}$ in. or $2\frac{5}{8}$ in.

One factor that some hunters never consider is the effect of recoil on their shooting. If recoil is so great as to cause flinching when the gun is fired, this can become painful and your accuracy suffers.

The amount of recoil depends primarily upon three factors: the weight of the gun, the weight of the shot, and the amount of the powder charge. The action of your gun also influences the recoil effect. Thus, some of the recoil energy developed in the semi-automatics is used to operate the mechanism, and this tends to lessen the effect on the shooter. Also, guns with fairly straight stocks (a minimum of drop at the heel) and with single barrels tend to have less recoil effect than those with a large drop at the heel or with double barrels.

To lessen recoil, try using lighter loads with less powder and shot. You can also install a rubber recoil pad to minimize the effects.

The heavier your gun the less is the recoil. The reason for this is that it is more difficult to accelerate and blow a heavier object backward than a lighter one. Thus, a particular shot charge used in one gun may leave your shoulder black and blue, but be completely comfortable to use in a heavier gun.

ELEMENTS OF SHOOTING

Almost every muscle of the body is brought into action in grooving the swing of the gun. The lower part of the body, including the feet, legs and hips, regulates the horizontal movement of the swing; the upper part of the body controls the vertical movement. Both parts must be brought into coordination to ensure a proper swing. This can be done properly only by shooting in a standing position.

As you stand, place your feet to face the shot, with the left toe pointed a little to the right of the exact direction the shot will be fired (for right-handed shooters). The right foot should be a few inches back of the left, with the right toe turned still farther to the right. The legs should be spread just enough so that the position you assume is completely comfortable. Most of the weight of the body should be upon the left foot. Any weight borne by the right foot is upon the toe, since the right heel can leave the ground as one swings. If the feet are close enough together, it is not necessary to lift the right heel.

After facing the shot, the lower part of the body is pivoted as you swing, but without moving the feet. The legs should be fairly straight without undue bend to the knees, though the knees should never be locked. The hips should be level so that the swing will be horizontal. This means that you should stand on a fairly flat surface so that you will not be thrown off balance as you swing. If the swing is higher in one position of the arc than the other, it is much harder to regulate the vertical position of your gun muzzle so that you are on target; it is also harder to keep an effortless balance as you swing.

The left hand and arm must be well under the fore-end of the gun to support and point it properly. The left hand and arm supply most of the weight and power for the gun swing. It is necessary that you grab the fore-grip well forward to enable you to point easily and comfortably. If your left arm is bent too much at the elbow, your gun will feel too heavy and will wobble as you swing. So keep that left elbow comfortably straight with only enough bend to make the grip seem natural. The right elbow should be held moderately high— not horizontal—but high enough so that the upper arm does not touch the chest.

Of great importance in accurate shooting is the position of your head and cheek. When the gun is brought to shooting position, the cheek should ride the comb of the gun stock. The cheek should be able to find this position as you move the gun up to your shoulder and as you dip your head slightly forward and to the right. If your cheek moves off the comb, the head lags behind the swing and the eye is not in proper position to aim the gun. This happens for right-handed shooters when the swing is to the right, since the gun is pulled away from the cheek and the sighting plane is disrupted.

In spite of what some shooters say about never seeing their gun barrel when they shoot, the best shots see their barrels by keeping their heads down. The muzzle of the gun serves as the front sight; the eye is the rear sight and its position in relationship to the muzzle determines where the shot will go.

This means also that uniformity in cheeking the gun is important. If one time you cheek the gun tightly and the next with head high in the air, there will be many unaccountable misses. There is sometimes a tendency to lift your head from the stock to see the bird, particularly on a second shot. So practice rapid shouldering, sometimes with your eyes closed, then looking to see how you are lined up. Keep at this until you can bring your gun up and with your cheek pressing the comb in one smooth, fast movement.

You should shoot a shotgun with both eyes open. Both eyes are needed to help you find and follow the target, to act as range and direction finders, and to enable you to aim the gun accurately. An experienced gunner follows the target with one eye and sights along the gun muzzle with the other eye. Using only one eye is actually a great disadvantage. He finds it hard to see both the bird and the gun muzzle with one eye; he has very poor depth perception and has trouble swinging on, and past, the target to insure proper lead. So if you have not already learned to do so, keep those eyes open while aiming and shooting.

The gun is aligned on the target by your "master eye." For a right-handed shooter this is the right eye.

To determine your master eye, align your finger upon some object with both eyes open. Close the left eye; if the finger remains aligned upon the object, your right eye is the master eye. If the finger moves out of alignment with the object, then your left eye is the master eye. Every gunner ought to hold his gun so the master eye sights along the barrel.

I come now to the important subject of how much to lead your target. This depends upon the bird's speed, whether it is crossing, quartering, going directly away or coming in; how far the gunner is from the target; and the velocity of the pellets. For example, using a standard 12 gauge express load of $3\frac{3}{4}$ drams of powder and $1\frac{1}{4}$ ounces of $7\frac{1}{2}$ shot on a bird traveling directly across the gunner's path at a speed of 60 miles per hour and at a distance of 50 yards, the computed lead is 15.2 feet. At 30 miles per hour at 50 yards, the lead would be 7.6 feet for $7\frac{1}{2}$ shot, and 7.0 feet for 9 shot. At 30 yards, the lead would only be 4 feet for $7\frac{1}{2}$ shot.

However, it is impossible for a gunner to estimate accurately distance, angle, and speed in an actual hunting situation. The gunner can use one of two styles of shooting to find the proper lead on moving targets.

The Fast Swing

The first style of shooting is called the fast swing. The gunner starts his gun muzzle behind the bird, moves the muzzle rapidly along the line of flight of the bird, past and in front of the bird, firing when experience tells him he is out in front enough. The important thing is to follow through, to keep the gun moving as you pass the bird and shoot. If you stop the muzzle, the time taken to stop, pull the trigger and for the shot to travel the necessary distance to the target, will allow the bird to move beyond the point where you are aiming. Most gunners who miss their targets are shooting behind the bird, not realizing that they freeze the gun after pulling ahead of the bird and before pulling the trigger.

It doesn't matter how fast the bird is going when using this method. The faster the bird, the faster you swing the gun as you pull ahead and pull the trigger of the gun. If a bird is crossing slowly, an easy swing will be sufficient to pass him and only a short lead will result by the time you pull the trigger. If a bird is moving rapidly across, the gun must be whipped past it, resulting in a longer lead when you pull the trigger. This system works regardless of how far away or close the target is, since moving the muzzle ahead of a bird a few inches will result in many feet of lead at forty or fifty yards, but only a foot or so of lead at very close ranges. Thus, lead is automatically adjusted.

The Sustained Lead

The second style of shooting, called the sustained lead, is used by many hunters for more deliberate pass shooting. With this method, the gunner starts his swing ahead of the bird, estimates the lead needed, and maintains his lead as he keeps his muzzle moving ahead of the bird along the angle of flight. The successful gunner with this method is one who continues to move his muzzle ahead of the bird and who can estimate the proper lead needed, and adjust this for various ranges and speeds.

Another style of shooting, called snap shooting, is used most successfully on nearly stationary targets. With this method, the hunter raises his gun to his shoulder, points at the bird (since the bird is not moving) and gets off a quick shot.

Be conscious of the flight angle and path of birds moving in different directions and how this effects your swing and lead. For example, one of the easiest-looking shots is a bird moving straight away. Yet, to follow the line of flight to make this shot requires you to move the gun muzzle downward along a vertical plane and to actually shoot under the bird. Conversely, a bird moving straight toward you requires you to move the gun muzzle upward along a vertical plane so that you actually shoot over the bird.

In shooting at a flock or covey, always pick out one bird to aim at; never shoot in the general direction of a group of birds. If you try this, the shot invariably goes between the birds.

In waterfowl hunting, flush the birds off the water before shooting. When a bird is resting on the water with wings folded, it makes a very low silhouette, the vulnerable under parts are protected, the heavy wing cover protects the upper parts, and so the bird is harder to kill than in flight.

In flushing both surface feeders and upland game, remember they jump vertically straight up off the water or land, then fly away. Wait until the bird has reached the peak of its upward jump, and shoot just before it moves off horizontally. If you shoot the instant the bird jumps up, you will usually shoot underneath the bird.

In hunting pheasants and other long-tailed birds, allow a generous lead. Over half the total length of pheasants is nothing but tail feathers.

Do some practice shooting before the season opens. Practice bringing your gun properly to your shoulder, placing your cheek on the comb. Practice your swing and lead at all sorts of moving targets (such as song birds in your back yard), and practice taking the safety off your gun and cocking your gun. If possible, practice shooting clay pigeons on a trap or skeet range.

12

Clothing and Special Equipment

THE CLOTHES you wear depends on the type of hunting you do and weather conditions. When hunting upland game, always wear brightly colored outer garments as protection against being shot by your own partners or other hunters. When waterfowl hunting, the more camouflaged your clothing is the better, since you must keep the birds from detecting your presence in order to get within shooting range.

WARM-WEATHER CLOTHING

Underwear—light cotton absorbent shorts and T-shirt.

Trousers—Light cotton pants or jeans are adequate unless you are tramping through wet or heavy cover. Don't wear heavy canvas or wool trousers in warm weather. Wear tan, khaki, or camouflaged colors for waterfowl.

Shirt—light cotton shirt, tan or camouflaged for waterfowl, bright red for upland game.

Cap—light summer cap with ventilating holes. Wear a light cotton, camouflaged cap for waterfowl, red color for upland game.

Footwear—for upland game, light, well-oiled leather boots with rubber or crepe soles. You can buy boots with 6-, 8-, 9-inch or higher uppers. I prefer the 6-inch for a lot of walking in warm weather in light cover.

HEAVY-COVER CLOTHING

Footwear—fairly rugged, well-oiled boots with rubber or crepe soles are best. I prefer the 8- or 9-inch heights for walking in heavy brush.

Trousers—double-faced canvas hunting trousers or leather-faced hunting trousers are best. In hot weather wear medium-weight jeans or army or navy pants.

Shirt—a medium-weight cotton duck is good in warm weather; in cold weather, wear wool underneath and a heavy parka or hunting jacket. The parka or jacket ought to have a rugged outer covering of cotton duck or canvas. Light nylon or cotton covering tears easily in heavy brush.

Gear laid out the night before the hunt helps the duck hunter get underway early in the morning. *North Dakota State Game and Fish Dept.*

WET-WEATHER CLOTHING

Footwear—use only shoe pacs (with rubber feet and leather tops) or rubber boots. When tramping around for upland game, I prefer the shoe pacs to either rubber or leather boots. They keep my feet dry but are still comfortable to walk in. When duck hunting, I prefer rubber boots, the height of the tops depending upon the depth of the water to be waded. Chest-high waders (insulated in cold weather) are best for deep sloughs. Hip boots are needed for water 2 or 2½ feet deep (insulated in cold weather). If I have to wade in water only inches deep, 12-inch boots are adequate.

Rain gear—if you are hunting in the rain, or tramping through high wet cover, wear a rubberized rain suit. I prefer suits with separate trousers (the kind that come up to the chest in front and are held up by suspenders) and separate parka-like tops. The top should have a zipper front and a hood. Outside pockets in the parka are handy.

Head gear—I prefer wearing a canvas cap with a long bill (to keep the rain off my glasses and out of my face). I put the cap on my head and the parka top over it.

COLD-WEATHER CLOTHING

Underwear—in very cold weather, I wear long knitted underwear with separate pants and shirt plus lightweight Dacron, fiber-filled padded underwear, or multilayer, padded underwear over the knitted. The warmest insulated underwear made is made by Duofold, Inc. This company sells 4-layer, quilted insulated underwear or 2-layer insulated underwear. The 4-layer is the warmest underwear I have found, even though slightly heavier than quilted, dacron, fiber-filled suits.

166

Dacron, fiber-filled, quilted underwear comes either in 3-ounce or 5-ounce weights. It gives a maximum warmth for its weight.

Trousers—heavy wool, unless you are tramping through briars or brush, in which case jeans, heavy duck pants, double-faced canvas or leather-faced pants are best.

Shirt—heavy wool is always appropriate. I personally prefer my Duofold, two-layer "Sportsman's Doublet." This is a very warm pull-over shirt with a wool outer layer and a soft cotton inner layer.

Parka—fiber-filled or down-filled Dacron parkas are the warmest per ounce of weight. Make certain the outer covering is heavy enough to withstand tearing and snagging. I prefer a parka with a cotton duck covering, to one with a light nylon covering. The parka should have a hood with a drawstring to keep it pulled tightly around the head.

Gloves—insulated mittens are warmest but must be removed to shoot. Gloves lined with foam rubber, fur, or wool are warm and comfortable, but also must be removed to shoot. Thin, tight, deerskin gloves or special shooting gloves which allow the trigger finger to protrude, can be worn while shooting, and are preferable for upland game hunting where speed of shooting is so important. In waterfowl hunting you can free your shooting hand when the birds are coming in, so any kind of warm mittens or gloves are wearable, provided they are loose-fitting enough to be slipped off easily.

Footwear—an oil-tanned, insulated, leather boot is best. Leather boots ought to be oiled regularly, or treated with silicone, to preserve and waterproof the leather. I always use insulated rubber boots to keep my feet warm in cold weather while waterfowl hunting.

This hunter's parka serves as camouflage as well as protection from the cold. *North Dakota State Game and Fish Dept.*

GUN CARRIERS

When transporting your gun it is well to have it encased in a special gun case. Cases are made of canvas, plastic, and leather, lined and unlined. The very light plastic is unsatisfactory because it tears; the heavy plastic and canvas are adequate and less expensive than leather; the leather is best but most expensive. The best cases have soft fleece inner linings.

GAME CARRIERS

Some hunting coats have rubber-lined game pockets in the rear or sides. Such coats are handy ways of carrying game, but ought never to be used in warm weather as game spoils readily in such pockets. Even in cold weather, do not leave the game for very long in the pockets; get your birds out in the air where they can cool off.

A better carrier is a canvas game bag with a web strap to go across the shoulder. Another fine way to carry game is in a special game vest with a lightweight canvas pocket in the rear. A light belt carrier, consisting of a metal ring on each end of a web strap, is a handy gadget. The head of the bird is slipped in the metal ring and the web strap is looped over the belt.

Special game carriers can be installed on the top of the car. This is usually an enclosed wire cage placed on a regular roof carrier. This carrier allows the birds to cool off as the car is moving along.

AMMUNITION CARRIERS

You can use either a webbed ammunition belt which buckles around your waist, or a special ammunition vest or coat. I prefer the belt since it is less of an impediment to shooting. Most vests hold more than a box of shells. In addition, some hunters prefer to carry their shells in the car in a metal ammunition box, taking them out as needed.

DOG CARRIERS

If you use a truck or station wagon for hunting, you can build or buy a plywood or aluminum dog carrier to fit in your vehicle. I use a station wagon and have built a plywood dog box with holes for ventilation and a hinged door, to fit in the rear of the wagon. It works beautifully and holds four dogs.

If you go hunting in a sedan, you will need a roof carrier to which a plywood or aluminum dog carrier can be attached. The same plywood carrier I place in the back of my station wagon attaches to the roof carrier. One summer, I carried three large labrador retrievers over 4,200 miles on the roof of my car. The dogs received just the right amount of ventilation through the wire door on the rear of the box and through the holes in the side. The front of the box, and the roof, are solid plywood.

Ducks are loaded into convenient car-top carrier. *North Dakota State Game and Fish Dept.*

MISCELLANEOUS EQUIPMENT

A compass is a necessary instrument to have whenever you go into unfamiliar woods, desert, or mountains.

Hand warmers feel good on the palms or kidneys on cold days.

A pocket knife to use in gutting or partially cleaning game comes in handy.

Topographical maps help in locating likely hunting areas in unfamiliar territory.

A flashlight is recommended if you are leaving before daylight or returning after dark.

First-aid equipment ought always to be carried along in case of accident.

Food and drink is a necessity on any trip. I always take along a thermos of hot coffee, or cold water, plenty of sandwiches, and candy bars or fruit. If you are going to be hunting in a dry area, be sure to take along some water for your dogs.

13

Hunting Dogs

THE VALUE OF A HUNTING DOG

The benefits of a well-trained dog to the day's hunt are many, and those benefits are not limited to strictly utilitarian functions. The handling, training, and use of a dog in hunting becomes a sport in itself, and the companionship and rapport that develop between a man and his dog can be understood only by another dog man. In order to develop a relationship of this kind, however, one must first have a genuine liking for dogs, and a willingness to cope in an understanding and patient manner with the problems inherent in dog ownership. Almost every man I have known who has failed to develop a dog to the level of an enjoyable and helpful shooting companion, has failed because he does not essentially like dogs in the first place. Many of these individuals love to see a good dog at work, but simply are not equipped emotionally to rear one themselves. It is extremely important to do some serious self-examination before you buy a dog; if there is any doubt in your mind, don't experiment on the dog; just don't buy one. On the other hand, if you honestly think you are the type who will enjoy owning a dog, and are willing to go to considerable lengths to raise and train it, get the pup of your choice, and you will never regret the investment in time and money.

THE VARIOUS JOBS DOGS DO

Before going into the details of purchasing a good dog of your selected breed, we should consider the kinds of jobs that dogs are equipped to do.

In the interest of consistently filling your game-bird limits, probably the most important job that the hunting dog can perform is to locate and expose birds to gunfire. This job is done in different ways by the different breeds of dogs. The pointers, setters, and Brittany spaniels find birds by ranging out, and freezing on point when the game-scent is strong enough to indicate that they have a bird pinned; that is, the bird has been so overwhelmed by the speed and suddenness of the dog's approach, that in fear, it elects to sit tight; and it will do so, under ideal conditions, until the hunter arrives to flush it out, or the dog is sent in to flush. This kind of dog work is restricted to the various upland game, and some species respond better to the work of pointing dogs than others.

The second type of game-finding is known as quartering and flushing. The spaniels, especially the English springer spaniels, are the experts in this line of work, and accomplish their task by running back and forth in front of the gunner, always within gun-range, routing and flushing the birds which in many cases would not have flown up to hunters without a dog. There is some dispute among dog men as to the merits of the flushing type of dog as compared with the pointing breeds, but it is generally conceded that some birds, in certain kinds of terrain, are worked more effectively by the pointing breeds and some by the flushers. There is no question, however, that any well-trained birdfinder will provide you with more shots on almost any upland game than you would get without a dog.

Another interesting use of the dog as a game-finder is in locating tight-sitting ducks, usually mallards, along the edges of sloughs, rushy creek beds, etc. The best dog to use for this work is usually one of the retriever breeds that has been trained to flush upland game. Retrievers are rugged enough to stand the prolonged exposure to cold water encountered in this type of hunting, and are usually careful, methodical workers, which are needed in hunting ducks that have decided not to move.

While finding game to shoot would seem to be the most important function of the hunting dog, with the exception of waterfowl hunting, an equally important function is the retrieving of downed game. In many kinds of cover it is practically impossible for the hunter to find downed birds without the aid of a retriever. Hunters who do not use a retriever kill more birds before filling their limits than hunters with retrievers; the implications for conservation are clear. In upland-game hunting, it is usually possible to train the pointing and flushing breeds to do a creditable job of retrieving, although most individuals of the nonretriever breeds require considerable force training, and very seldom retrieve with the verve or accuracy of the retrievers. A notable exception to this is the English springer spaniel which has been bred for generations for its retrieving as well as its bird-finding instinct. For duck hunting, it is practically imperative that you get one of the retriever breeds, a Labrador, golden, or Chesapeake, as these are the only breeds that can be relied upon to work out as water dogs with some reasonable surety. The retriever breeds have heavy protective coats, strong bodies for swimming and endurance, natural alertness, and the good eyesight required for this kind of work. Above all, try not to be overly impressed by the champion of his breed who claims that his is "the all-around breed." Invariably, the all-around dog is barely adequate in several departments, and excels at nothing. I would rather take my chances with a real specialist, basing my choice on the kind of hunting that I do most, and hope that I could train him to work passably on game of lesser interest.

HOW TO BUY A GOOD PUP

The first and most important factor in selecting a breed is to consider the game that you will hunt, primarily. Obviously, if you intend to hunt ducks and geese in the cold northern states and Canada, it would be ridiculous to buy a Brittany spaniel; on the other hand, it would be equally foolish to buy a Chesapeake for bobwhite hunting in Georgia. If you have the idea that your hunting will split about evenly between an upland species and water-fowl, choose the breed that you know can handle the toughest of the two assignments, and try to "make do" on the other. The retrieving breeds, for instance, are very popular in the northern part of the country because they can stand the cold water in duck hunting, and at the same time do a creditable job flushing and retrieving pheasants in the manner of a spaniel. By the same thinking, many hunters in the warmer parts of the country, and even some of these in the North, prefer one of the German pointing breeds, or the springer spaniel, since all of these breeds, while bred primarily for bird find-ing, are also bred and expected to retrieve from land and water. Climate is important in the selection of a dog only with regard to the kind of weather and water conditions he will be expected to work in. Any of the hunting breeds will survive the coldest winters or the hottest summers if they are given good kennel facilities, and the proper feed and care.

Next in importance to selecting a breed that will be able to do the job you want it to, is to select a breed you have a natural inclination and admiration for. We all have our likes and dislikes, and, irrational as they may be, they should be considered in selecting a breed so that you don't get a dog you are only lukewarm about. Don't be too concerned about price; all good pups cost money, and a pup of good breeding in the breed of your choice that costs a lot more than a scrub is worth the additional money in the long run. You needn't lose much sleep over the question of temperament, since, regardless of the reputations the various breeds may have, almost all well-bred hunting dogs have been bred for generations for tractability and good disposition. It is indiscriminate and unselective breeding which produces vicious, shy, or untrainable dogs. Choose your pup intelligently from any of the hunting breeds, and the chances are extremely slim that you will have any trouble with disposition.

If you are not very familiar with the working style and nature of all breeds, the best thing to do is to limit your field of choice to two or three of the breeds that are known to have the qualifications you are after, and put in some time, and travel if necessary, watching the best performers in these breeds work. The best way to do this is to observe their work in field trials. After you have seen them all work you will no doubt form pretty positive opinions as to which breed will serve your purposes best.

Another excellent source of information and advice in selecting a pup, or a breed, is the professional trainer or the top amateur handler. These men know their dogs exceptionally well since they depend on this knowledge to win, and are usually quite generous in pointing the beginner in the right direction, if they are convinced of his sincerity.

UPLAND-GAME DOGS

The pointers and setters must be regarded as the chief upland-game dogs. These breeds, especially the pointer and the English setter, are the ones in which we find most of the "big going" rangy quail dogs of the type that are followed on horseback in the field trials of the South. There are strains, however, within both of these breeds which are bred to work closely, or at medium range, and are intended for the hunter on foot, and for less open country. It is impossible to generalize about the two breeds, or maintain that one is better than the other. So much depends on your needs, and the individual strains from which the dogs come. One can resort to field trial statistics, and demonstrate to the satisfaction of some, that the pointer is the better dog of the two; yet the English setter may be adapted to some jobs more adequately than the wide-ranging pointer. Weight of coat, appearance, temperament, and other factors may cause the prospective dog buyer to choose the English setter over the pointer in some instances.

An English setter has helped these hunters bring down two ringneck pheasants. The English setter is one of the two chief breeds of upland game dogs.

The Irish setter and the Gordon setter also belong to the pointing group, but are less numerous than the pointer and the English setter. Both of these breeds have been taken over largely by the bench fancy, and a few generations of breeding without paying scrupulously close attention to working ability can result in an almost total loss of the hunting instinct. If you want an Irish or Gordon setter, be absolutely sure that you get a pup from a known hunting strain; you then stand a reasonably good chance of getting a decent dog. If you make your selection strictly from show stock, you stand about as much chance of getting a hunter as if you had bought a Pomeranian.

There are several breeds of pointers known as German pointing breeds, among these are the German shorthair, German wirehair, and the Weimaraner. The Hungarian Viszla, though it is not German, in physical char-

The German shorthair, an all-around pointer, has been bred to hunt small-animal game as well as birds. *North Dakota State Game and Fish Dept.*

The Weimaraner, one of the German pointing breeds, is shown here with a bag of sharp-tailed grouse. *North Dakota State Game and Fish Dept.*

acteristics and working style belongs to this group also. All of these dogs are billed as "all-around" dogs. On the European continent they were bred for pointing, retrieving, and trailing small furred game. This multipurpose role stems from the European tradition of hunting multiple game species in the same outing, and is reflected in such other items of their hunting equipment as the German drilling, a gun with a pair of shotgun barrels and a rifle barrel mounted in the center below them.

The American tendency has been to breed away from the all-purpose dog, which is a slower more plodding type dog, and toward the flashier, more rangy class bird dog type. Most of this development has been initiated, and is being carried out by the field trial people, and, in my opinion, they are getting a better type of hunting dog for most of the conditions in the United States through this program. I think, at the same time, that we must recognize the long distance these breeds have to come before they will reach the level of class ex-

A black Labrador retriever with a mixed bag of mallards and honkers. His thick black coat provides excellent protection from the water. *North Dakota State Game and Fish Dept.*

hibited by the best pointers and setters, if that is what they are after. The German pointing breeds supposedly have more retrieving instinct and require less training than the pointer and the setter. I have seen a rather large number of individuals of both breeds, and have owned some of each myself, but have failed to substantiate this opinion in my own experience. If anything, I have seen a rather inordinately large percentage of hard-mouthed dogs in the German breeds. This may be the result of a rather strong infusion of hound blood which was introduced in Europe in an attempt to improve their scenting qualities.

Among the breeds developed primarily for use on upland game, there is probably more diversity among the spaniel breeds than any other. There are the springer spaniels, English and Welsh, field spaniel, cocker spaniel, English cocker spaniel, clumber spaniel, Sussex spaniel, American water spaniel, Irish water spaniel, and the Brittany spaniel recognized by the American Kennel Club. Many of these breeds have been taken over by the bench fancy, and some are practically extinct on this continent. Unless you are particularly drawn to an exotic or rare breed, select your pup from a breed that is represented in fairly large numbers; you have much more to choose from, and usually much better dogs. If I were considering a spaniel, unless I wanted a pointing dog which the Brittany is, I would go no farther than the English springer spaniel in my search. This breed is the most highly developed for field work in this country, and is the master breed for pheasants, one of our most popular game birds. I have seen several springers turn in really re-

A wet golden retriever receives a pat of thanks for his efforts. The golden is a favorite of many. *Michigan Conservation Dept.*

spectable work on ducks, too, and if I were to buy any other breed than a retriever for that job, it would be an English springer.

The spaniels have a natural tendency to quarter, or work back and forth in front of their master, and usually are very tractable and easily trained to work in this way. A well-trained dog of this type will look back to his handler frequently, checking his range, and taking special care not to put up any birds out of range. In this respect, the spaniels are totally different from the pointing breeds who range out, locate their birds, and hold them until the gunner arrives. Without question, a spaniel which is not trained to work closely will put up most of his birds out of range, and is far more of a detriment to the hunt than an asset.

RETRIEVERS

The retrievers are probably the most specialized and highly developed for their task of all the sporting breeds. Retrieving instinct, build, water-going instinct, soft mouth, marking ability, memory, alertness, desire, nose, bird interest, and many other essential qualities have been bred into these dogs for many generations. Of the several recognized retriever breeds, only the Labradors, goldens, and Chesapeakes remain in any significant numbers in this country. The Irish water spaniel, which is considered primarily a re-

A Chesapeake Bay retriever swims home with a catch. The Chesapeake stands cold water better than most other retrievers.

triever, the flat-coated, and the curly-coated retrievers are so scarce as to make looking for a good one in this country a practically impossible task.

The Labrador is the king of the field trial game, and is numerically the strongest retriever in American Kennel Club registrations. There are many good strains of Labs which produce offspring that are fast and aggressive water dogs, with the natural style and ability to make top hunting and field-trial dogs. The coat of the Lab is an excellent deterrent to water, as it is hard and flat on the surface, with a glossy, oily finish, and a dense woolly undercoat which seals off the skin from the water almost perfectly. The Lab is known throughout the world for his excellent disposition, and a snappy one is an extreme rarity. Many Labs are so out-going and tractable that they can be successfully handled in field trials by just about any competent handler that knows the commands. Labs come in several color variations: black, yellow, various shades of golden or chocolate are accepted colors, but black is by far the predominant color, and almost all of the really good ones are black. If you want a Lab, you might as well plan to own a black dog. Many Lab owners maintain that the color of a dog is of no importance in the blind, and that ducks pay no attention to a dog anyway. I have found on several occasions that a dog will scare off ducks that are decoying, and if your dog is black, you simply must make every effort to completely conceal him from view while hunting. I have a Lab myself, and use him in the duck blind a lot, as well as in field trials, but I use an extra-heavy blind which conceals both hunter and dog.

The golden retriever would receive the votes of many as the most handsome of the retriever breeds. In general, the conformation of the golden calls for about the same type of dog as the Lab. The distinctive difference in these two breeds is the coat. The golden has a bushier, longer coat, with a somewhat silkier texture, and as a rule, luxuriant feathering on the tail, hindquarters, and underparts. The golden's coat is in large part responsible for his good looks, and provides excellent protection against cold weather. A disadvantage of this long coat though, is the fact that it has a tendency to hold rather large amounts of water, and is not quite as good protection against this element as the Lab's and Chesapeake's. The coats of most goldens do have a good dense undercoat, though, and one selected from good water-working parents is likely to make a real water dog himself. Some of the breeders of goldens are working away from the excessively long coat in an effort to make better water dogs of this breed.

In general, the golden retriever is perhaps a little slower than the extremely flashy and exuberant Labs. This cannot be interpreted as a hard and fast rule, however, as many of the hardest going, best marking retrievers I have known have been goldens, and the dog that stands out in my memory for the best water entry, both on marked birds and blinds was a golden retriever. Golden retrievers are not nearly as common as the Labrador, and they do not win as many field trials, but if you have your heart set on a dog of this breed, and you get a pup that has a background of good stock, you won't regret it.

The Chesapeake Bay retriever is the only American native of the retriever breeds; the golden and the Lab are both of English origin. The Chesapeake was bred by the bay men and the market hunters of the last century, and was expected to endure the hardest work under the most adverse conditions that a retriever could be called upon to do. Much of this ruggedness and stamina has been retained through careful selective breeding, and if a really tough dog is what you need, the Chesapeake might be for you. Many people mistakenly think that because the Chessy is so rugged, and somewhat aloof, that he is surly or dangerous. I have owned several dogs of this breed, and have known many others, and while many of them put up a good bluff if they think an intruder is on their premises, I have never owned nor seen one that would bite. They usually have very even and dependable dispositions, and when they know a stranger is alright, are usually very friendly toward him.

On the whole, comparatively few Chesapeakes compete in field trials, but the few that do have been quite good and seem to do at least their share of the winning and placing. This breed is subject, perhaps, to wider varia tion in physical type than the goldens and Labs. Some strains of Chesapeakes are extremely large, slow, and methodical in their work; and the best of these are very dependable performers but lack the style and drive for field-trial competition. Other strains of the breed, like the good strains of Labs and goldens, are of medium size, are fast and aggressive, and have all the style and verve that could be asked for. Again, it can be seen to be very important to select your pup from individuals within the breed that have the characteristics you want.

The coat of the Chesapeake is perhaps its most distinctive feature. The coat varies in color from the darker shades of brown, to a very light dead grass. Almost any good Chesapeake color is good camouflage, and one of the arguments for this breed is the color of their coats. In texture, their coats are usually very hard and oily to the touch, the undercoat is of a dense, woolly consistency, and is also very oily. Perhaps one of the reasons for the relative decline in the Chesapeake is the quality of his coat—when he gets wet, he gives off an unpleasant smell, similar to a wet sheep. I don't view this quality as a shortcoming myself, as the Chesapeake is the most favorably equipped of all breeds to work in cold, wet hunting conditions. Many of these dogs can stand in icy water all day long, and show no apparent discomfort. Most Chesapeakes are very quiet, patient, and pleasant to spend a long day in the blind with; more so than Labs, who seem on the whole to be a bit more excitable and nervous.

While the main function of the retriever is to bring downed game to hand, one should not overlook the possibility of using them as quartering and flushing dogs. Most of the retriever breeds will work out very well if trained to work in this manner. They are big and tough enough to keep going all day long, and their dense coats protect them from the briars and heavy cover in which birds like to hide. Most retrievers are endowed with exceptionally fine noses also, and this is a prerequisite in any good flushing dog.

HOME CARE

The minute a man takes possession of his puppy or dog, he should consider it a binding contract to give him the best feed, kennel, and care that he can provide. Before the new dog is brought home, the kennel should be constructed. The best arrangement is a concrete run, about 4 feet in width by 20 feet in length. A pen of this size will allow the dog room to stretch and move about. A heavy-gauge fence of at least 6 feet in height should surround the concrete, and a good-sized, double-walled and insulated dog house should be placed outside at one end with a hole cut in the fencing so that he can get in and out. The dog house should be provided with clean bedding frequently, and should have a heavy flap nailed over the door in the winter to keep out the cold. Once you know your dog is safely confined, and will not be running around town getting into everybody's hair, and since the kennel floor will be cleaned daily and your dog will be trained not to bark, your neighbors will have no reason to complain. It will be found that an extra bonus is to be had by keeping your dog kenneled when you are not with him; he will have more energy and desire to work for you when you take him out than if he were left free to roam around all day.

REARING AND TRAINING

Rearing the new puppy is probably the most critical stage of dog ownership. At this time in life, as in human beings, lasting impressions will be made. Your dog will either learn to trust and respect you or to be fearful and apprehensive in your presence. Animal psychologists have shown that dogs must be socialized between the ages of five and eight weeks, or there is very little chance that they will be able to establish the necessary relationship to man during their entire life. You must get your pup young, then, do nothing to make him mistrust you, be lenient but consistent, feed and water him with the utmost regularity, and try to see that no member of your family does anything to make the pup fear man. Contrary to popular belief, the dog can and does generalize; if he encounters a bad experience with man early in life, the chances are that this will establish a fear in him of all men. The better your dog knows you, the more tractable and eager to please you he will be, and this is a great asset in a hunting dog. There is no better time to get to know your dog than when he is a pup.

The training of a dog should begin with very brief but frequent lessons as a young puppy. The span of interest in an eight-week-old pup is very short, but he is able to learn a few simple commands even at that tender age. I like to start my pups on obedience and field work at about eight to ten weeks, or immediately after the pup is well acquainted with me. Most of this work amounts to little more than play, but the repetition has a way of making an especially lasting impression on the young dog. There is great danger in overworking the pup, and you must be absolutely sure not to put a lot of pressure on the young animal, nor use methods of severe punishment, as you will only cause him to fear you and hate his work. As the puppy matures into a dog, you will be able to see how much work he can stand and still enjoy it. Try not to exceed this limit in the first year of the dog's life, and you will always have a happy, vigorous worker, enjoying a job well done.

Dogs, like men, must be in good condition to do a hard day's work. If you are training your dog daily, or at least three times a week, the chances are that he will be in close enough to good condition that it will take him only a few days of hard hunting during the season to achieve really top condition. If, for some reason, your dog has had a considerable layoff previous to the hunting season, take him out regularly three to four weeks before the hunting season opens, and run him in the country behind your car, or better, behind a bicycle, and you can get in shape too.

The best performing hunting dogs are those who are in training the year round. One excellent way to keep your dog in shape the whole year, and provide a bit of fun and sport for yourself in the bargain, is to run him in field trials, of which there are many held throughout the country each year for the various breeds. These trials will give you some notion of how good your dog really is, since most field-trial competitors are examples of the best in their breed. Trials are held for most breeds at the formal, or licensed, and informal level. It costs lots of money to campaign a dog on the licensed trial circuit, and it certainly does not pay if your dog is not top flight. On the other hand, informal trials are held for most breeds, and often the competition is made up of some of the top winners in the nation.

Most field-trial tests are set up to resemble as closely as possible an actual hunting situation, although usually the tests and the work done by the dogs is far beyond anything the average hunting dog could do. Whether you run in field trials or not, the trial game is responsible for a large share of the development and improvement of our sporting breeds. Field-trial men select nothing but the best for breeding stock, and in this way perpetuate the top bloodlines which carry the traits we want in a sporting dog.

Index

Index